PRO SE PRISONER:
GUÍDE TO
BUÍLD
WEALTH

Masters of Money

C.A. Knuckles

Freebird Publishers

Box 541, North Dighton, MA 02764
Info@FreebirdPublishers.com
www.FreebirdPublishers.com

Copyright © 2024
Pro se Prisoner: Guide to Build Wealth Cryptocurrency, Real Estate, & Business
By C.A. Knuckles

All Freebird Publishers titles, imprints, and distributed lines are available at special quantity discounts for bulk purchases for sales promotions, premiums, fundraising, educational, or institutional use.

ISBN: 978-1-952159-48-0

Printed in the United States of America

- **DEDICATION**

To those lost in the cycle of poverty, incarceration, and poverty-stricken ghettos. Behind me is a strong woman who has pushed me to do great things. I will never forget the role you played in my success. I love you, and thank you!

• ACKNOWLEDGEMENT

Thanks to Freebird Publishers for their support. All the people who helped with this book's research took a year to complete. And all the prisoners who became pro se prisoners by purchasing my last book, Pro Se Prisoners: Guide to Build Wealth. Continue to support, and I will continue to provide knowledge.

Thank you. The Forgotten Voices!

CONTENTS

REWARD

INTRODUCTION

Welcome back to part four of the Guide to Build Wealth series. Part four is called Masters of Money, which provides more steps on your financial literacy journey. My goal has always been to provide value to your life by giving you financial knowledge so you can build wealth. If you haven't purchased my last books:

Pro Se Prisoner: Guide to Build Wealth [Credit & Investing]

Pro Se Prisoner: Guide to Build Wealth [Taxes & Banking]

Pro Se Prisoner: Guide to Build Wealth [Cryptocurrency, Real Estate, & Business Forming]

All can be purchased from Amazon.com or FreebirdPublishers.com. Make sure you spread the word that Pro Se Prisoner books are the go-to resource for financial knowledge and wealth-building strategies. Our next quest brings us to part four of Guide to Build Wealth [Masters of Money]. It shows you the ways the wealthy generate money and control the output of it. This is not about people who have mastered money, such as Robert Smith (the wealthiest black person in the U.S.). It is about what products, services, and strategies you can use to Master Money. Look around any catalog with books, and you will see a lot of financial books about Warren Buffet, J.P. Morgan, etc., but none of them show you how to be a Master of Money yourself. Quickly, understanding how to do it yourself is a process; it requires you to think about creating industries while not forgetting that our goals have to align with ways to reshape the neighborhoods from which we came. The greatest value that I can add to your life right now is giving you the knowledge and information to succeed at your goals.

Masters of money know that their time is an investment. It has a price because time is precious. Poor people will always measure time in relation to money, while the wealthy measure their time. Poor people have really always valued money more than their time because they lack the financial literacy to Master the Money that controls them. So, to become a Master of Money, we must answer this simple question:

What are your core values?

1. _____

2. _____

3. _____

Take some time and think about it because once done, you will see mentally where you are as a man or woman. If you list things that relate to street life, like I am a gangster, real, a go-getter, etc., it's fine because once you read this book at the end, you will answer these same three questions again. Your values and beliefs will change. Understanding how to become a Master of Money will clearly be defined.

WHAT IS A WEALTHY MINDSET?

Q: What is your definition of a wealthy mindset?

A: _____

_____

_____

_____

_____

_____

_____

Pro Se Prisoner Answer: A wealth mindset is not just about getting rich. It's about building a foundation for your future and creating an environment that will allow you to grow your wealth. It's important to understand that wealth building is a process, not an event. It takes time, effort, and consistency to build wealth.

Your answer shouldn't be considered right or wrong because all we are trying to do is get a mindset check on where you are from the start so that by the end, you become a Master of Money and not a slave to it. So, wealth or becoming wealthy starts with your mindset.

WHY IS BUILDING WEALTH
IN PRISON IMPORTANT

Building wealth while in prison has many benefits. Prisoners with strong financial literacy are likelier to find employment or start a business after release and are less likely to return to crime. Prisoners who save money while incarcerated are more likely to have a successful transition into society and not return to jail.

It is important that prisoners have access to financial literacy programs so that they can grow their wealth while incarcerated. These programs teach prisoners how to manage their finances, build credit, and get out of debt when released. Building wealth in prison has a number of advantages.

The first advantage is that prisoners have an opportunity to learn about money management and the importance of saving. They can also learn how to budget their money. They will also learn how to take their savings and invest from prison.

Another advantage is that learning the banking system and being able to set up an outside bank account allows prisoners to earn more interest on their money than they would otherwise earn in a prison-owned account provided by D.O.C. Lastly. However, some prisons have offered some form of financial literacy programs through partnerships and non-profits, but 95% still don't, and that's the greatest public safety threat to society.

Not providing these programs and sending prisoners home unprepared restricts jobs and causes the recidivism rate to be in the 70% percentile year after year. Over 70% of crimes committed in the U.S.A. involve some financial component. So why not fix the problem?

The American prison system is in need of a major overhaul. One of the biggest problems is that prisons do not offer inmates the opportunity to build wealth. This needs to be at the top of the agenda, and that needs to change. Prisoners are limited in what they can do for work and money-making opportunities. They are also not given access to many financial literacy resources, which have led to a few problems:

1. Recidivism Rate above 70% (year to date)
2. Crime in Prison
3. No Rehabilitation
4. No Financial Re-Entry Programs

Looking at these problems, you can see why the United States is the world's largest incarcerator, with more than 2,200,000 people in prison or jail. The prison system is supposed to be designed to rehabilitate prisoners and turn them into productive members of society. However, it has been found through research that prisoners are not able to prepare for their future because they lack financial literacy adequately. While they tell prisoners they can't invest, no laws prohibit investing or even opening a bank account if signed over by a Power of Attorney Form or by starting an LLC while still in prison.

Our prison system is broken and is a big contradiction of its own doing. It's not just overcrowding, the violence, or the lack of rehabilitation. It's also about the lack of opportunity for people to learn how to build wealth while in prison. Developing financial literacy builds a strong foundation for a better future. You can build years from prison. There are many obstacles that can make it difficult for prisoners to attain financial stability on the outside and even more so on the inside. Such hindrances include a lack of education and a lack of understanding of how money works. Providing a basic understanding of how money works helps prisoners make smart decisions about their finances and improves their chances of securing a well-paying job. Although the Pro Se Prisoner way is building your own company that provides value, some of us can still use a high-paying job to help finance our plans upon release.

So, why is building wealth for prisoners while in prison important? It's not just about building wealth for prisoners. Being financially literate helps them get out of debt, manage their money better, plan ahead, and invest. It also helps prisoners set clear financial goals designed with concrete plans. Furthermore, businesses have been created on the backs of prisoner labor, forgetting that communities have sprung up from deserts, rural areas, and abandoned towns. While also creating industries that have been built around prisons and prisoner labor. This is why the opportunity to build wealth is so important.

$

BECOMING A MASTER OF MONEY
WHILE INCARCERATED

Incarceration can be difficult—an uncertain time in your life. But that doesn't mean you have to sit by idly as your life passes you by. With the right strategies, you can come out of prison wealthier than when you went in. Here are some tips on how you can become a Master of Money while incarcerated.

- **Saving Money & Money Management**

The first tip for building wealth while incarcerated is to save whatever money you have coming in, Which may sound obvious. Still, it's quite difficult to do when living in a prison cell, especially with limited income and available resources. To make saving easier, set up a budget and track your spending so that you know exactly where your money is going each month.

Pro se Tip: (!)

$100,000 a year, is just $273 a day. Make that and in 12 months you will have $100,000 – that simple.

This will help ensure that you're not wasting potential savings opportunities.

DAILY
SPENDING LOG

DATE	ITEM	AMOUNT SPENT	NEED	WANT
			☐	☐
			☐	☐
			☐	☐
			☐	☐
			☐	☐
			☐	☐
			☐	☐
			☐	☐
			☐	☐
			☐	☐
			☐	☐
			☐	☐
			☐	☐
			☐	☐
			☐	☐

INVEST WISELY

Another tip for building wealth while incarcerated is to invest wisely. Writing this today, I see that society is scared of a recession, high inflation, etc. Real investors are cashing in on current conditions because they have the knowledge and money to capitalize on this recession; the current economic conditions have triggered a recession. The U.S.A. government doesn't want you to know that, but this is why you have me to show you and tell you about these Master of Money economics.

It's a recession! According to all data points that measure these events, we are in a recession, regardless of what the news media and government officials say. They can't hide data points that show the strength and weakness of the U.S. economy. Before you can "Invest Wiseley," you must look at the economic forecast, such as the "yield curve."

The "yield curve," specifically the inverted yield curve, means short-term bonds have a higher yield than long-term bonds, which is abnormal. When the yield curve has inverted, it is followed by a recession; on average, a recession will start 12-13 months after the yield curve initially inverts. The yield curve is inverted, more than it has been since 1980. This current inversion started in July of 2022. Why is this happening now? Because the all-powerful Federal Reserve controls short-term bond yields, they have pushed them higher aggressively over the last year to fight inflation. Could the yield curve un-invert? Yes, but only if the FED cuts interest rates. And that will only happen if it's a massive slowdown because of interest rate hikes or a recession pushes them to do so.

So, the Federal Reserve can cause a recession and have the power to slow inflation! Think of that for a moment. You must expand your knowledge to know how to position yourself to capitalize on these economic collapses. The FED can grow economic activity in our country and worldwide or cause its collapse systematically.

Investing wisely during these troubling times must be backed by multiple data points. Think of all the financial books you have read over the years or those you have heard of; none of them talk about this type of advanced financial literacy provided in this book series. Some of these data points are put out by the Federal Reserve and economic institutions associated with the Government; all you have to do is know where to look and what to look for. Let's begin with the "savings rate." These are per-household rates, which are normally around 8%-10%. Right now, as of the writing of this book in March 2023, there is a 3% savings rate per household. Remember that 70% of the economic output in the U.S.A. is based on consumer spending. Dropping savings rates means consumer spending is going to slow down, which will slow the overall economy. Decreased savings due to inflation means things cost more, and people can afford less. Inflation decreases the amount of your $ dollars while pushing the cost of goods higher. The savings rate will help you know what 70% of the country's economic output is doing.

Housing prices are another data point. It's good to check mortgage rates and supply and demand dynamics. Mortgage rates will or have in 2023 drift down slowly. The supply and demand data shows demand has vastly outstripped supply for the past five years straight. We have been at a long-time low point for inventory because of high demand. This shows a strong real estate market, unlike in 2008, when supply was high and demand was low. The C.P.I. (Consumer Price Index) shows the inflation rate, but the wealthy look deeper into these inflation reports by focusing on the data around the "Core C.P.I.," which takes the "C.P.I.", which takes the "C.P.I." and stripes out of the effects of gas and oil prices, as well as housing or shelter prices. If the Core C.P.I. comes in above 5.5%, stocks will get crushed. While looking at these data points for investing wisely, also remember that under the above data points, the FED usually increases the interest rates. But if it comes in below 5.5%, stocks could rally on the other side.

When investing wisely, you must look at all data points. Becoming a Master of Money requires more than your daily stock readings. Understanding data history of past ups and downs across asset classes during these high inflation and high interest rates. Key points:

- The worst performing asset class during a recession is "S&P 500"

- The best-performing asset class has been bonds, which have averaged a positive 7.5% return over (3) three recessions. However, the downside is that bonds tend to struggle with inflation as the FED seems to continue raising interest rates to slow inflation.

- Gold has been one of the best asset classes, with a +0.7% return over three recessions. But the real plus about gold right now with high inflation is gold generally helps in an inflationary environment.

- Real estate REITs averaged -9.3% over (3) three recessions. But if we are still in an inflationary environment, that's a strong indication to invest in REITs (Real Estate Investment Trusts), which trade like stocks on the open market. The real estate market is strong because of strong demand but low supply.

- The worst-performing asset class is stocks, which averaged 17.3% over (3) three recessions. This shows you how sometimes data points can be negative but present the best opportunity. Usually, during the recession, stocks drop, but this is the best time to buy top stocks at bargain prices. Your job is to catch the stock right before it bottoms out, which is generally before a recession ends; the returns are explosive. Data points show that the best ten days in the stock market happen all the time in or around recessions, with a +8.4% in a day.

- Investing wisely across these asset classes can be achieved by investing in "Multi-Asset ETFs." These include stocks, bonds, commodities, and real estate all in one. Some to include in your research are:

1. iShares Core Aggressive Allocation ETF (AOA)

2. Cambria Global Asset Allocation ETF (GAA)

3. SPDR SSGA Multi-Asset Real Return ETF (RLY)

4. iShares Core Moderate Allocation ETF (AOM)

5. Wisdom Tree U.S. Efficient Core Fund (NTSX)

6. iShares Core Growth Allocation ETF (AOR)

7. Pacer Wealth Shield ETF (PWS)

Review all necessary data points beyond the basic stuff you read in the paper or hear on TV. Understand that your outside contact can send you this information by telling them to Google "Yield Curve," "FED Interest Rate," "C.P.I. Inflation Rate," etc.

Pro se Tip: (!)

TAX STATISTICS show:

In 10 years, the Treasury has collected $32 trillion dollars in taxes, Warren Buffet's company Berkshire has paid $32 billion dollars which accounts for 1% of the overall taxes collected by the Treasury. While it collected $32 trillion, the U.S. National Debt surpassed $31 trillion dollars. The data behind these debt number shows net interest payments in budget as shares of **GDP** are low.

Building wealth starts with changing your mindset. Those who want to keep you poor and in a prison cell, financially insecure, do so by convincing you that wealth and systems are complete and hard to achieve. They are not!! As you sit there in your cell, home, etc., reading this book, becoming a Master of Money requires only that you have the most knowledge about financials and have the expertise where you understand:

- Investments

- Taxation

- Structures

- Deal Making

- Debt

Once you understand these fields, you gain access to deals and opportunities others don't get; you gain leverage based on trust from people who will pay you for your financial expertise. Masters of money position themselves at the front in order to invest wisely and build wealth.

WEALTH OF KNOWLEDGE &
WHAT YOU CAN LEARN

Limited knowledge equals limited choices. Expand your knowledge so that you have more choices. Masters of Money learn new things every day to expand their financial options. While incarceration may be a daunting, isolating experience, it is also a place to gain solitude and plan while educating yourself 24/hours a day. Look at your isolation as an advantage you have over the rest of society. You have 20 hours a day nonstop to set goals, plan, and obtain knowledge, most times without distractions. What you spend your time on, you become. Time is your greatest asset; keep that in mind when you generate your plan because, as you will see, having a plan allows you to direct your time precisely and work smarter.

So, let's expand our knowledge while seeing what can be achieved and seen when you have the knowledge to see through poverty traps and take action based on it that helps you build wealth. Most banks have a slogan that says, "Come save money with our bank." Having a poverty mindset means you would save money in the bank in the long term. But being as though you are a Master of Money, you know that banks really don't tell you the truth about the money you place in their banks and other financial institutions. Some fall victim to the "Fractional Banking Ponzi Scheme" that prints money on demand, then loans at 100% of your money, giving banks a 10x+ plus on your money. Why would you save money when they profit at will? During the COVID-19 economic collapse, citizens of the USA didn't realize or see the data points that changed in March 2020. Banks are no longer required to keep any of your money in reserve (10% was the previous number). They literally take your $$$ and immediately lend it to someone, earning them up to an extra 10-15% on your money while giving you 0.01-0.05%. It is nothing more than a collective investment scheme that functions like a legal Ponzi Scheme that makes them billions of dollars, but if you or I did the same thing with people's money, we would be in prison for a very long time.

The Federal Reserve consists of 12 district banks, but the U.S. government does not own these 12 banks; other banks own them; they get paid a dividend of up to 6% of what the district banks make. The Federal Reserve Board in D.C. is a formal Federal Agency that the banks do not own. This Federal Reserve Board is the government agency that controls the interest rates in the U.S.A. Now you see why the U.S.A. controls the banks but doesn't own them, thus making them more powerful.

Pro se Tip: (!)
The value of becoming valuable. We are paid for the value we introduce into the economy.

One simple hack to beat the banks at their own game is with mortgages. Loans are the best way to beat the bank. Banks want you to pay mortgages monthly because of compound interest. Beating the banks requires you to stop the compound interest. (Example: If you pay $1,000 a month, pay an extra $30, this means you just pay $1 a day, which will equal to the $30 extra, $1 a day. Paying a dollar a day allows you to have 100% of your mortgage payment ($1,000) directly to your loan amount; you won't pay interest, or rather interest will never be deducted from the $1,000, because the $1 a day tricks the system to make it think you made a payment every day which will reset the interest portion of the system, thus allowing 100% of your payment of $1,000 to go directly to the loan to pay it down faster. Thus, a 25-year mortgage can be cut down to 5 years.

It's important to remember that you must have a variable rate, not a fixed rate because Fixed Rates are locked in. Fun fact: this hack against banks can be done with "credit cards" and "car loans" (which must have variable rates). This strategy aims to ensure you don't pay the bank interest on these loans and pay off your loan a fifth of the time.

Pro se Tip: (!)

Mortgage is a Latin word: Mort=Death; Gage=Pledge.

Signing a mortgage is a death pledge to the banks because a majority of people will never pay off a 30-year mortgage (i.e. Death pledge). But using a wealthy mindset, you now know how to get a variable rate mortgage that can be paid off a fifth of the time.

Beat the banking system by using the tricks that keep you financially trapped against them. Remember, mortgages are death pledges with you and the banks; they know you will never pay it off, which creates a lifetime interest payout for the bank. Always get a "variable rate" because it drops the interest rate to 0% by paying $1.00 a day and then paying the monthly payment on top of that on the monthly due date. The $1 a day will change depending on your loan amount, so do the math such as:

Example:	$383,461.46	-Loan Amount
	$. 1,556.55	-Charged Interest
	OLD Rate 5.12% / New Rate 5.37%	
	$20,591.88 a year / 12 months = $7,715	
	$7.715 / 31 days = $55.35 monthly	

Take the example of $55.35 and break it down again to see how much you will pay daily for 31 days.

Now, why are we talking about banks? It's something else equally important that you should know, plus this leads us into the next part of this book about "Trust" and "Insurance."

B.O.L.I. = Bank Owned Life Insurance

Yes, banks own life insurance; as of 2020, 3,137 banks nationwide owned B.O.L.I. 67% have assets between $100 million and $1 billion and currently own BOLI. There is 184.6 billion BOLI cash value on banks' finances as of 2020. (More on cash value later.) Quick Note: Banking is 100% about control of people, markets, and financial institutions. One of the ways banks use your money

---

Pro se Tip: (!)
Top 5 Banking Families of the World

1. Rothschild – started in 1760
   - RIT Capital Partners plc
   - Rothschild & Co. Bank
2. Junius and J.P. Morgan – started in 1813
   - $2.1 Trillion in Assets
3. The Warburg's – started in 1870
   - Wells Fargo / Federal Reserve Board 1914
   - Paul M. Warburg
4. Amadeo Giannini – started 1870
   - Founded Bank of Italy, which became Bank of America. One of the first people to offer banking services to the middle class.
5. David Rockefeller – started early 1700
   - Net worth 3.3 billion at death

Is buying life insurance, which is used for tax shelters and a way to fund benefit plans. Premiums paid into the fund, in addition to all capital appreciation, are tax-free for the bank. Therefore, banks can use the BOLI system to fund employee benefits on a tax-free basis. Here is a list of some of the biggest banks that own B.O.L.I.:

- Bank of America $24,037,000,000
- Wells Fargo Bank $19,369,000,000
- J.P. Morgan Chase Bank $12,115,000,000
- PNC Bank $10,572,902,000
- Truist Bank $7,515,000,000
- U.S. Bank $6,113,011,000
- Citibank $5,299,000,000

Remember, this isn't business insurance you would get for tangible assets, etc. This is the life insurance that these Banking Institutions purchase. These plans provide sources of income for the business, along with helping with executive compensation, thus producing tax-free income. As a small business, you can take advantage of these insurance policies, just as large businesses do. Now that you have made it to the 4th part of this book series, you should understand how to start a business, what business you want to start, etc. Just like BOLI, there is

COLI (Corporate Owned Life Insurance), which will be key for you when your business grows and key employees emerge. Getting C.O.L.I. on key employees will insure them and ensure that financial losses due to unexpected deaths of these key people will be compensated. At the same time, the company will build up the cash value to invest and pay executive compensation tax-free. Banks and corporations have used the insurance system to create and build wealth tax-free for generations.

Pro se Tip: (!)

$100,000 dollars a year is just $247 a day x 365 days = $100,000. It's that easy and simple.

Understanding the real banking system will allow you to create wealth by becoming like banks, using your personal and business money to build wealth properly. Financial institutions tell you what to think, like the crazy idea of saving money in their banks. Instead, you need to learn how the system works so you can take advantage of it. Life is an illusion. What you see is based on your beliefs. Optical illusion! Whatever your mindset is, you will see abundance or lack and limitations. Most people always seem to see a lack because you're feeding your mindset a lack! You're being programmed. Becoming wealthy is about a mindset change, not money!

Now, banks leverage your money to benefit their needs, so why not use the leverage of their money for your financial needs? One thing is certain: banks will give a dog money just to collect interest every month! So, leveraging the bank's money is simple; it requires getting a loan (a business loan is better) and using the interest as a tax write-off, thus providing you with a free business loan that creates a perpetual money cycle. So even if your business receives a loan with an "APR" of 5% or 6%, or 10% on a $100,000 dollar loan, that's $10,000 interest you're ultimately paying out. If personal, you pay out of your personal bank account, while if it's your business, you will have to pay that $10,000, but at year-end, you will be able to use that $10,000 as a write-off, which will lower your taxable income, which in turn allows you to pay less in taxes. This is the difference between a wealthy mindset vs. a poverty mindset.

Pro se Tip: (!)

50% of Americans earning over $100,000 a year are living paycheck to paycheck.
- U.S. Treasury 2022

Interest, loans, and credit cards are banking tools that will put you in bad debt or allow you to have good debt and build wealth. Quickly, yes, there is good debt! If you read the previous three books in this series, then you are aware that it's "good debt" that the wealthy use. For example, the wealthy will borrow money from the banking system, which becomes debt. Then, tie that debt to an asset that's going up in value, thus creating what's called good debt. Let's take it up a notch: you can pay off bad debt by using good debt. Or use debt to invest, which takes financial education. Being able to finance 100k with $20,000 down and it appreciated by 10%, you can make a 50% return on money. This is called increasing return on debt. Now, back to the start of this paragraph…. Bankers create recessions and trigger inflation and deflation. Right now, we are in a recession, as mentioned previously. Still, overall, when bankers create more credit/debit than can be used or employed in the economy, thus creating more money running to a few goods and/or services, inflation becomes a no-brainer. Deflation happens when the banking system pulls back the amount of credit created, thus deflating financial activity and employment. Our goal here is to handle the knowledge about this system so we can plot, plan, and execute when these data points are shown across the banking sector. Take a moment to understand this: we are in 2023; technology is so advanced that once hidden data about economic activity is opened on the internet or exposed by people within these institutions. So, stop making excuses about why you don't know something!

Real estate is another area where the wealthy use debt, loans, and interest.

The power of debt in the real estate context allows borrowers to gain full control over the asset by using other people's money. More importantly, you get the benefits of revenue, appreciation, and depreciation. Because our currency is a depreciating asset due to inflation, the wealthy appreciate assets such as real estate, which they can control. Here is an example of a good real estate deal using debt (loan) to purchase an asset.

- $100,000 – Value of House
- $80,000 – Seller sells it to you for
- 20% Down = $16,000
- 80% Leverage from Bank $64,000 – Debt
- 5% Interest Rate
- 30-year period = 30 year
- Monthly Payment of $344

The above example gives you control of:

- Revenue
- Appreciation
- Tax Advantages
- Business Deductions
- Tenant Rent: $1,200/Month

Use the tenant rent to pay the mortgage down $344 (debt), which is amortization at work. Now, you can clearly see how the wealthy used to pay off debt and use real estate's tax advantages to offset debt payments.

Becoming a Master of Money requires you to stop using a poverty mindset to justify why you aren't using the above wealth strategies to succeed. Poverty is not just a lack of financial resources but a state of mind that can lead to a lifelong cycle of struggle and hardship. A poverty mindset is a set of beliefs and attitudes that limit individuals from reaching their full potential and achieving financial stability. It's a mindset that views the world as lacking and sees opportunities for growth and prosperity as scarce. Many of us grew up in poverty-stricken environments and developed these mindsets, which can be passed down from generation to generation. Remember, the word "economy" comes from the Latin word "Economia," which means "the study or lack." This means you cannot have an economy if someone isn't lacking.

THE FLOW

Wealthy ⇓ Poor   Wealthy ⇑ Poor

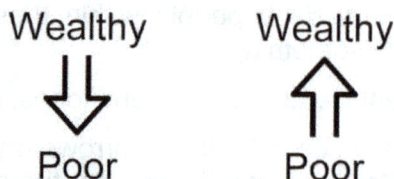

An economy must have flow for it to exist. The moment you find an equilibrium, you can't have an economy. There is clear data to show that people in poverty "Lack" financial resources and everything else that creates the poverty mindset that holds them back, but just know that it was designed/set up this way. Use this book series to get out.

Masters of Money are connoisseurs of information and ideas. They understand that the game is to use information to build wealth, and thoughts used to get wealthy are two different things.

GETTING: Requires confidence

STAYING: Requires humility

In real estate, information is important, and strategies are developed out of proper information; one of the best strategies Masters of Money uses is:

B.R.R.R.R.

Buy, Rehab, Rent, Refinance, Repeat

The BRRRR method starts off differently than you are used to. Traditional real estate investing tells you to go to the bank and get a loan to purchase real estate. With this method, you start by paying cash for the property rather than financing it. So, the **B=Buying** means that you are putting the money up to buy the property. **R=Rehab**, whatever work needs to be done to the property, you will need to put more into it to fix up the property. This process also adds value to the property, which is simply building equity. The investor does these first two steps. The goal of these two steps at the start is to add value before seeking financing through traditional means. Next, **R=Rent**, once the rehab of the property is done, you need to put it on the market so it can be available for tenants to rent, which begins your journey to build up cash flow. Because you spent the money in the beginning to purchase and rehab the property, your cash flow for the proceeding months will be high due to you not having a mortgage on the property. Create several months of positive cash flow, typically between 3-to-6 months before completing the next step. Let's dive into this renting process really quickly. Several books I have read about successful people who use this strategy always talk about the following:

- **The 1% Rule**

If your property is rented for $1,000 and you pay $100,000, this is 1% of the purchase price. So, this rule shows you how to price your rental based on the property's purchase price. This rule needs to apply to lower-priced properties in the $350k and under range. Because a $600,000 property won't command $6,000 in rent to be profitable, the less the property is, the better this rent strategy works.

One thing I try to remind myself when seeing people use these strategies is not to try to copy other successful people but to Master Money, understand why what they do works, and then find new ways, developed through action, to utilize those new strategies in your life.

Now, back to the BRRRR Method. Now that we got the B.R.R. out of the way, let's go straight into the R=Refinance; in order to do this step, we must go to financial institutions. The refinanced amount is based on the value of the property after it has been fixed up. Traditional financing is based on the value of the property before it is fixed up (lower). Thus, the reason the B.R.R.R. Method is better is that you finance when you fix it up when the property is worth more. These banks are valuing your property based on the fixed-up value, which means you will get to pull more capital out of your project because you chose to finance it after adding value. Lastly, **R=Repeat**. This is probably the simplest part of the B.R.R.R. Method. By this point, you have developed relationships with key people in your industry, thus allowing you to be more efficient in the future when repeating the process.

Now, some strategies associated with the B.R.R.R. Method are good and work great but combining them to complete this process is more effective.

- **Buying Key Points**

As mentioned previously, 1% of the purchase price works best for properties being purchased under $350,000, which will give you control of guaranteed cash flow from the property. Another point mentioned previously is that the wealthy deploy 75% of ARV, which will allow you to regain 100% of your capital. Most real estate investors will tell you about buying multi-family properties first; that's okay, but remember, these are valued based on their N.O.I. (Net Operating Income) along with the capitalization rate of the surrounding area. Improving the N.O.I. is the way.

Pro se Tip: (!)

Velocity of Money: how many times can you buy an asset with the same dollar.

You should focus on increasing their value. Single-family homes' value will increase when you improve their condition because the value is based on comparable sales in the area where the house is located! One key element of the buying process is the numbers, mainly:

- Acquisition cost
- Rehab Cost
- ARV

Once you understand these numbers at the outset, you will instantly know if your potential property will make money. When you are buying property, keep an eye out for all those that require a cash offer. These offers have a way of putting you in front of the seller and pushing out everybody else.

• Rehab Key Points

The most important point of the rehab process is having a top-tier "Contractor" you trust to get the job done on time and on budget. Select the best contractor, and don't settle for just past results. Study it but rely more on the contractor submitting an "itemized bid" describing the activity, scope of repair, rate, and cost. This will allow you to see their vision for your property. Remember, this rehab process will add value to your property from the outset; focusing on the bathroom, kitchen, and new appliances will allow you to add the most value to your property, which always gives you a better return on your investment and better rent %'s.

• Rent Key Points

Remember, the best metric for property under $350K is the 1% rule. The rent should be 1% of the sale price to achieve this. Doing rent by the 1% rule allows you to take the guessing out of the process. Also, all economic data about the surrounding areas, such as employment, ongoing development, etc., should be taken.

• Repeat Key Points

In order to repeat this process, you must have your team in place to act on any new deals, so you are repeating the buying process. The B.R.R.R.R. Method is about the consistency and velocity of money. With this repeated process, we are looking for the repeated application of the process that allowed you to close this first real estate deal.

Other areas of the. B.R.R.R.R. Method that may be bought up through your research of these different aspects of this method includes:

Using Other Financing

You can buy these properties without using your own cash! This includes borrowing private money; Using hard money loan that allows you to buy, rehab, and upon refinancing, you can lock into a long-term loan with better advantages; using a HELOC (Home Equity Line of Credit) on rental property; Taking a business loan out using your LLC credit score (Paydex); and lastly you can use seller finance for the short term, this allows the owner to become the bank and hold a mortgage note against their property.

Now, understanding this concept of B.R.R.R.R., you can see how the wealthy develop systems around existing financial laws and banking systems to build wealth in the long term. The beauty of this process is it allows you to buy properties every 3-to-6 months, each time using the previously bought properties equity to buy double the properties you bought before. Refinancing helps you out in the end because you can increase the loan amount and withdraw the money, which can be used to buy more real estate; as mentioned previously, when you take out debt against an asset, it's tax-free. What also happens is that your R.O.I. (Return On Investment) is greater than the interest that you pay on the debt. Pulling equity out of your property is tax-free because you receive it in the form of a loan, which cannot be taxed. With cash-out refinancing, remember you

Pro se Tip: (!)

When starting or forming a company, use the following words at the end of your business name upon forming, so you can get high limit funding. Certain names will get you better funding than others:

- o [Company Name] Consulting
- o [Company Name] Holding
- o [Company Name] Enterprise
- o [Company Name] Worldwide
- o [Company Name] Technology

can pull out at least 50% of the value of the property once appraised. Get to work.

CREDIT BUILDER ACCOUNTS
& CREDIT HACKS

Since the last three books, I've found more accounts that allow you to build credit while you are in prison. All you need is an outside trusted person to set up the account.

- **KOVO**: This program allows you to build credit by having an address and SSN. It costs $10 monthly for 24 months.

- **TOMO**: Allows you to build credit with little money.

- **CREDIT HACKS**: Utilization Rate: Pay down to 5% or less at least five days before your "statement date." Call your credit card company and ask for your "statement date." It's usually the end of the billing cycle, so pay five days before that. Your utilization accounts for 30% of your score so that you could control 165 points.

- **BEGINNER CREDIT CARDS**:
    - Chase Freedom Flex [No Annual Fee]
        1. Apply for a Chase bank account (one or two months before applying for a credit card.
        2. Apply for Chase Freedom Flex
        3. After 2-3 months, apply for a Cash Sapphire card - $95
        4. If you know someone with Chase, ask for their referral link.
        5. If denied, call the "reconsideration" line. 800-945-2006, press "0". Ask them to consider you again and ask for the reason for the denial. Work it out.

- **CREDIT BUILDER ACCOUNTS**
    1. Trygrain.com – Easy loans
    2. Meetava.com - $72/year / $6/month

        $56/year / $9/month

They also have a build credit and some options that allow you to pay $21/month for 12 months. Each payment of $21 builds a payment history, which is 35% of your credit score. Plus, you also save $252 in the process that you get back at the end of the 12 months. Another option is a digital credit card with a $2500 limit that you pay back as you use the card if you apply a bank account to it for autopay. So, you can have two different credit types reporting from one company, each showing a positive payment history. MeetAVA is a good place to build credit, with just your SSN, name, address, and link to a bank account.

- Cred.ai: is another such credit builder. It's like a debit card used to build a credit payment history. You put money on it like a debit card, which becomes your limit. Once you purchase something with the card, it deducts like a debit card but reports to credit bureaus once you make the purchase, thus showing a positive payment history.

- Pen Fed Credit Union:

  1. Open a PenFed checking account (800-247-5626) or online.

  2. Add $250 to the account.

  3. Wait 30 days and open a "Share Loan" (Secure Loan) with $250.

  4. Pay it off in 6 months with payments of $41.

  5. APR is around 2.05%

  6. Build credit and relationships with PenFed to access their high-limit funding.

Also, Navy Federal has a similar program called a "Navy Federal Pledge Loan" that has similar features. Still, it's great for building credit and accessing Navy Federal higher-limit credit cards. These credit unions want to do business with you and form a relationship. So, you will have to put money in a Navy Federal Savings account for up to 30 days. Thus, you are required to set up a checking and savings account beforehand.

MASTERS OF MONEY

STARTING A TRUST

Sometimes, as a prisoner, I question what I'm doing. The hours, all day long, writing, reading, and purchasing books over the years have sometimes taken their toll, but every time I feel like I'm slacking, seeing how financially deprived prisoners are talking about finances in prison has put a spotlight on me. On an average day, multiple prisoners and officers alike seek out financial advice from me; my reach has pushed out of these bars onto the streets. One thing that I've found out is that correctional officers are just as lost financially as prisoners. We are in prison serving a sentence. They are working for the prison system, so, in essence, we are both caught up in the prison system. Both don't have a clue about financial literacy; one knows the prison system deprives you of financial education (prisoner), and the other doesn't believe that because they work in a system that pays them over $100,000 a year (Maryland). But I don't think it's only that. Both have generations of people who believe the same thing. This financial literacy problem is generational! Because I'm a prisoner, I'm often looked at by prison officials as just that, a prisoner! They want to know how I can talk about finances better than the people they claim are financial experts, whatever a financial expert is. Oh yeah, plus I'm black and have been in prison since I was 15 years old, almost 19 years now.

To be honest, I never really understood my power, talking about finances, or my ability to speak clearly and simple financial terms and strategies to people until a prisoner told me about a credit hack. He overheard me tell someone else in the hallway how he did it and raised his credit score to 620 from nothing in 2 months! Also, he said, "something so complex, broken down so simply." Another example was me explaining in 4 steps how to purchase real estate without using your own money to an officer, and to this day, they have done it five times and now have seven properties within years. I realized I had to do something better with my financial knowledge; that way, it could reach more prisoners. But doing all this, I started standing out; thus, I was being held to unrealistic standards, so a little mistake in prison became a big issue because of who I am.

My goal is to create generational wealth and give out generational knowledge to anyone who will listen, mostly to prisoners sitting in a cell, about to be released, or who are home on parole or probation. My obligation to them is more about inflation, recession, high-interest rates, etc., going on right now. All that is ten times worse for prisoners because private contracts overcharge us for simple stuff. So, to create generational knowledge with generational wealth starts with knowing how to pass it to the next generation or your family. That starts with understanding what a "Trust" is and how to set up one.

- ## Basics of a Trust

Trusts are based on "contract law," not "legislative law." This means that governments cannot take property owned by a trust because governments can only regulate and tax entities it creates (legislative law); because trusts are based on "contract law," the government doesn't have the authority over what's in there if it's set up the correct way. Even when it comes to taxes, under IRSC 643B, you can defer capital gains or keep them in the trust bank account. Because of this, selling everything to the trust allows the trust to pay for all of it using tax-deferred money. You are allowed to sell all your assets to the trust. Again, it must be set up correctly and written out in a contract, including all IRS codes, laws, and provisions; not doing this allows the trust to be attacked!

Pro se Tip: (!)
Generational wealth is wealth that is passed down from one generation to the next.

There are three types of trusts that are used in the U.S.A.:

1. Revocable Trust (Living Trust)
2. Irrevocable Trust (No changes)
3. Testamentary Trust (Activates upon death)

Under Revocable Trust, it has to be created while the granter is still living. An **Irrevocable Trust** cannot be altered after the trust has been created. Your will creates a Testamentary Trust if the will instructs for a trust to be created after you pass. You can obtain a lawyer or use simple methods like LegalZoom.com, select "personal," and plans start at $279; it will take you through every single step. Personally, I would obtain a lawyer who specializes in setting up trust accounts because you want your contract to include every aspect and provision you need to build wealth through the trust properly. Remember, we are setting up this trust to build wealth now, thus passing down generational knowledge and wealth.

Building wealth is a part of becoming a Master of Money. Another way to do this with trust is to use life insurance to fund it.

- ## Trust & Life Insurance

As you sit in prison physically, many prisoners and everyday citizens are guilty of "Lack of Financial Literacy." One of the most common people that prisoners talk about when it comes to getting rich is Robert Kiyosaki's "Rich Dad, Poor Dad." That book has been so successful around the world, giving hope and lessons to people in a financial prison. He teaches you how to make money while telling you about assets and liabilities. But the wealthy is different. While "Rich Dad, Poor Dad" tells you how to make money, it doesn't tell you how to become a "Master of Money." These lessons explain to you the process of not making money but making money create itself, using the same dollar as many times as possible, setting up trusts, life insurance, private equity, and becoming your own bank! To do these things, I have to go beyond the traditional talking heads; we sit around, listen, and buy their books. Creating generational knowledge allows you to pass down this financial mastery, not just generational wealth. Your parents and grandparents never passed down generational knowledge because they didn't understand money, the power of debt, taxes, and life insurance to build wealth. This is your chance to learn how trusts and life insurance, when properly structured, can lead to generational changes in your family tree forever. In 2023, data and information will be more like the world's new currency. How you use this knowledge and data points is key; you must execute!

What is your understanding of what life insurance is? Most of the people in America think it's a death-only product. In order to keep you financially disadvantaged, you are generationally trained by the school system, etc. So, in order to keep you buying life insurance as a death product, they allow you to be confused, so long as you never get that it's really a lot of tax-free money in it. Growing up in Baltimore City, life insurance was only for funerals, and there were a lot of those growing up. Half of the people with life insurance are underinsured, thus speaking to the confusion. It's simple why it's called "life" insurance if it was for only funerals. I refuse to allow you not to get this generation's knowledge that needs to be passed down to future generations. Now, there are three types of life insurance:

1. Term Life Insurance
2. Universal Life Insurance
3. Permanent or Whole Life Insurance

Based on the above types, insurance companies use a pricing strategy that includes:

1. Mortality
2. Internal Administrative Expenses

Term Life Insurance is a contract where the insurance company provides coverage for a specific number of years. They usually use a fixed rate of payment for a specific duration. Upon death, your beneficiaries will be paid the face value of your policy. The insurance cause is always so cheap because Term Life Insurance usually means you will outlive the term, but you most certainly assume all the risk, which is good for the insurance company.

Pro se Tip: (❗)
98% of all term policies written in the USA never paid a claim.

One example of such a term contract would be if you have $250,000 worth of term life insurance as coverage for, say, a 15 to 20-year period if you die.

Within that period, the insurance company will pay $250,000 to your beneficiary. Here's the trick: if you die past the 20th year plus a day after the policy expires, that same insurance company will not benefit your family. With term life insurance, your coverage stops when the term expires. They get all the money you spend, with the added slap in the face of no benefit being paid to your family.

Universal Insurance is a permanent life insurance contract that offers similar protections as term insurance but has a savings component that provides one of the best aspects of life insurance, "Cash Value." This form of life insurance was created in the 1980s to go up against the stock market. Keep in mind that 90% of insurance policies never pay out a claim, so why do most Americans have them if the insurance companies reap all the rewards/income? We will talk about that more later. Having universal Life Insurance, always keep in mind that these policies vary from insurance company to insurance company. There are two important parts of these policies. The first is the cost of life insurance expenses, which include annual renewable costs and administrative fees associated with the policy. Secondly, there are savings on investment discounts, which also carry additional management fees. You will have a guaranteed amount of death protection, and any excess funds will move into the savings component, which bears interest. [i.e., Cash Value] While also allowing you to grow cash on a tax-deferred basis.

The difference with Universal Life Insurance is that all the components included, such as the cash value, premiums, and coverage limits, more than likely will increase or decrease within the policy. Other forms of Universal life Insurance are:

- Indexed Universal Life has two parts. Part one covers the cost of life insurance expenses. Part two is your choice of guaranteed or non-guaranteed, with an option to tie to major stock market indexes like the S&P500, Nasdaq 100, and Russell 2000.

- Variable Universal Life Insurance Variables also carry two parts. The insurance expense being one and part two being separately managed accounts, part two being separately managed accounts, referred to as sub-accounts or Mutual Funds

Whole Life Insurance is probably the most common of these three types of insurance policies. This policy guarantees payment of the death benefit to your beneficiaries in exchange for premium payments. You pay the premium as you live, and your policy builds the all-important cash value. Cost can be high because the insurance company assumes more risk due to the guaranteed pay cut.

The cash value part of the policy is the second part of the policy, or the "savings portion," with this. The trick is to ensure that the whole life insurance policy includes a "dividend" paid out to you. That dividend is important because when it's declared, it will increase the cash value and the insurance death benefit. Once declared, it is so powerful within the policy that it can never be taken back. Cash value and its importance in a policy can't be minimized once it starts accumulating. It does so on a tax-deferred basis. Next, adding a "supercharger" paid-up addition rider allows you to get the chance to increase policy and death benefits by increasing the policy's cash value.

Understanding the importance of life insurance is important for this section on trust because it allows for the accumulation of tax-free money to invest that can be passed down through several generations.

Pro se Tip: (!)

IRS Codes associated with life insurance:

- IRC 101(a): Death benefit transfer tax-free.
- IRC 72€: Money grows tax-free within your cash value life insurance policy.
- IRC 7702: Money is accessible tax-free because of the policy loan provision.

The government loses more than $80 billion a year due to life insurance! Before we get into trust and buy life insurance, let's teach a history lesson about an important person who connects the most powerful families in the world.

E.F. Hutton was a powerful person in financial circles. There was even a saying people used to mutter about him. Which was: "When E.F. Hutton talks, people listen." By showing the IRS tax code, he found a loophole that said that if you buy any amount of life insurance, you can stuff it full of cash and have that completely off the IRS radar. Because Mr. Hutton walked in the circles of the wealthy, he called up the Rockefellers, Kennedys, and Rothschilds to inform them that he found something that would protect their money tax-free from the IRS. After those conversations, these families were putting $100 million dollars in life insurance policies in 5 years.

Now you know when the powers that be, such as the government, which ironically wrote these laws, got knowledge, then Wallstreet found out, rules were put into place to slow the wealthy down. These rules were centered around how quickly you could fund these policies; what they were doing was genius at the time because they were buying $10,000 life insurance policies and, at the same time, putting $100 million dollars in them. Wow! Soon after, congress changed this by adding that you must always have more death benefits than you have cash. The strategy they used was to take out small life insurance death benefits and put in the most premium allowed, which, at that time, you could have more cash value than the death benefit.

Remember, life insurance is part of building generational wealth. By using cash-value life insurance policies, you can accumulate cash value over time. We are securing the future generation's financial future. Next, we combine the power of a trust and life insurance together using a trust that owns life insurance on your family members, allowing you to have your wealth centralized, directed by a trust that gives you the power to control your wealth instead of the government. This is called becoming your own bank, gaining interest, cutting out the traditional bank, and creating one for your family. Just because you're in prison, don't think that this can't be accomplished. I'm living proof life insurance can be bought while you are in prison. I made this knowledge available at the end of the book series because this is one of the last steps of the wealth-building process.

Setting up the trust is the first step, and then you appoint yourself as trustee. This gives you complete control over the assets. Next, get your family together and inform them that the family trust will purchase whole life insurance for all trust beneficiaries. This policy will have a strong cash value, and once this happens, they can borrow money from the trust (beneficiaries) based on businesses they want to start or invest in. The trust will be the beneficiary of the life insurance policies. Upon death, the death benefit replenishes the trust tax-free. You get the benefit of your money, tax-free. The goal is to put your businesses in there for a 1005 write-off for specific entities. Upon death, the company or estate gets the death benefit tax-free, minus what you borrowed against the death benefit, as you are making money moving around. Another point to remember is that never put your child on the deed of your house; instead, put the house in the trust, as this will protect your child from being liable for any gains over time because he would have to pay taxes on it.

- **Everything is in the trust!**

The benefits of allowing the trust to own assets (i.e., business) and life insurance together are taxes! Assets are owned by the trust now, so the money coming in from real estate or other businesses is using the EIN of the trust, not the original business's EIN from your LLC. Because the government can't tax entities it didn't create, that's the main reason you can defer the money in the trust. Now, you can get all the benefits of write-offs because you don't own anything anymore.

Also, deferring taxes in perpetuity means that you are deferring it in perpetuity. In simple terms, when and if you make a distribution, you never pay taxes when the money is in the trust. But this is only if you use the money for a legitimate trust expense or when providing a benefit to a beneficiary; tax won't be paid on that money "due to legitimate trust expenses."

If by chance you were to distribute money out of the trust, an example of this would be issuing a "K-1" to a beneficiary or drawing a "1099" as a trustee, then the taxes change, and you would pay taxes on that money. Usually, the wealthy use the "demand note" to avoid that. This is what I mean when I tell you that "generational knowledge" is much more important than passing down generational wealth because the knowledge creates the proven process that allows you to take action to build wealth through multiple generations.

Combining a trust and life insurance is the way to become your own bank. Having assets under the trust it owns is another way to generate tax-free and deferred wealth.

Briefly, insurance has survived for hundreds of years. It is the only product that has survived the Great Depression and the Great Recession without a collapse. Life insurance dates back to 1760. No financial crisis affected these companies.

Pro se Tip: (!)

Stock Life Insurance Include: Hartford, MetLife, and Prudential. Mutual life insurance companies have no shares to buy like the above, you are in essence a shareholder in the insurance company if you are a policyholder.

The most important thing to take away is that insurance is the key to the trust. So, how do we take complete advantage of the insurance part of the trust? Ensure you get the lowest amount of "death benefit" your insurance company offers. This is because you will need to over-fund your insurance policy on a consistent basis. It's best to get whole life insurance so you can overfund it. Commissions can be lowered when you over-fund because that cash that's being pushed in goes straight to cash value rather than the premium. Don't allow an agent to put together a policy that doesn't allow this. Usually, they try not to allow this for up to 3 years at the start of the policy. They usually don't allow you to be able to pump up the cash value for several years.

Remember not to get discouraged or confused when sitting in your prison cell or living room. Generational knowledge requires you to understand/comprehend these seemingly complex terms, which will allow you to properly pass wealth down, build wealth now, and not pay taxes.

Pro se Tip: (!)

71% of Americans overpay in taxes each tax cycle.

You are able to complete this over funding by utilizing a little-known process called "paid-up additions." This means these additions are defined as "extra money" being placed in your insurance policy to pass the required contractual obligations. When you do this, the goal is to grow your cash value, but in essence, you also grow your death benefit. It's all in the contract, so it's important to have everything spelled out. In the first year, you can have cash value amassing at 30% to 40% of the money put in the policy. Cash value build-up has a limit; never go over that limit because your tax benefits will be lost. We are building wealth while mastering money, but at this po, it's about a legacy, generational knowledge, protection privacy, and tax advantages that grow completely on a tax-deferred basis. Loans taken out of your insurance are tax-free. Even the death benefit that grows cannot or never be the subject of income taxes. If that's not enough, remember your policy earns a dividend yearly.

Using a trust correctly with life insurance allows you to create a bank for your family, which you can borrow from and replenish, using life insurance to keep it replenishing every generation. If one generation uses the money, their death benefit will allow it to be put back tax-free.

Our goal is to Master Money and Build Wealth using Generational Knowledge while passing down Generational Wealth with the know-how to protect and grow whatever family wealth is left to you. Prison creates a mental prison that doesn't allow you to look past your circumstances, see the real side of life, and build wealth while you are in prison. Not that simple shit like going home and getting a job, but legacy shit! Keep reading my Pro Se Prisoner books, take the knowledge, and take action. If you are reading this, you don't need pep talks because you should have taken action since book 1, so let's continue. Starting with a trust that buys whole life insurance to build cash value and borrows tax-free, upon death your death, the benefit replenishes the money taken out, while the asset you purchased is accumulating income that goes into the trust and gets deferred because the trust owns it, and not by you. Plus, you are using the trust EIN for tax purposes, not your LLC's original EIN so that you can defer taxes on that income coming in. By the trust using IRS 643B, capital gains can be deferred. While also allowing your trust to set up and buy life insurance and putting the trust as the beneficiary.

While also allowing your trust to set up and buy life insurance and putting the trust as the beneficiary of the life insurance policy (whole life insurance). Thus, it allows you to give generational knowledge while forever passing down generational wealth and opportunity for each generation after you! Remember, money follows value!

• **Forming Your Holding Company**

When completing your trust and buying your life insurance policies, it's a good strategy to form a holding company to maximize your tax write-offs and separate your assets from you even more. The wealthy use this strategy; as the picture below shows, it's a three-level tier of protection. Our goal to Master Money and build wealth must start with the don't own anything, control everything!

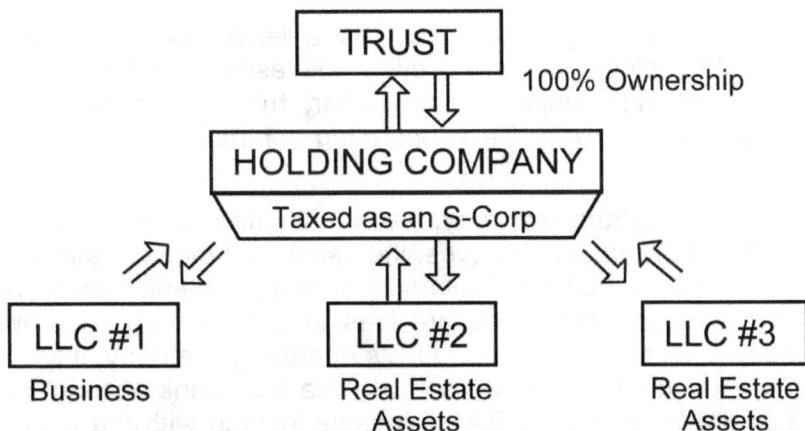

```
                    ┌──────────────┐
                    │    TRUST     │      100% Ownership
                    └──────────────┘
              ┌────────────────────────────┐
              │    HOLDING COMPANY         │
              │    Taxed as an S-Corp      │
              └────────────────────────────┘

   ┌──────────┐      ┌──────────┐      ┌──────────┐
   │  LLC #1  │      │  LLC #2  │      │  LLC #3  │
   └──────────┘      └──────────┘      └──────────┘
    Business        Real Estate        Real Estate
                      Assets             Assets
```

The trust has 100% ownership of the holding company (taxed as an S-Corp), the holding company owns the assets of your LLCs (main businesses), and when your business pays a dividend or income, it doesn't go to you directly, it goes to your holding company, that the trust owns 100% of, thus allowing for tax-deferred income. Your trust will also have the life insurance policies created earlier, plus your personal residence, cars, etc.

A holding company of this type only intends to perform business activities such as borrowing, lending, and making investment decisions. It will also loan funds or lease assets to an operating company that will carry out certain business activities. While there are several benefits to having a holding company set up this way with a trust, the most common benefits of a holding company include tax reduction and asset protection.

Setting one of these up requires you to choose a structure out of two known structures, such as an LLC or a Corporation. Once you choose the structure, file your formation documents with your state agency and set up a bank account assigned to your holding company; remember, the owner of this holding company will be the trust that you set up first. The trust will have 100% ownership of the holding company, so remember to name the trust as the owner of the holding company when setting up the structure with the state agency for such an application. Obtain an EIN before going to the bank. A perfect company with easy filing is www.incfile.com. Select the plan that is most desirable to you. Stop! The first thing to do is to set up a virtual office because you are going to need this address to give to Incfile so they can send it to your state agency. One of the best virtual business address companies is Opus Virtual Office. You can also build your business profile and business credit card with each payment to Opus. They will report it to the business credit agencies.

Remember, the holding company controls the assets, so if you have an operating company already, such as an LLC, that's doing business and producing income, you are going to now file a "transfer of assets," selling all of your valuable assets of that LLC, such as real estate, equipment, intellectual property, and commercial real estate, to the holding company. Keep the account separate. Each company should have separate accounts for this transaction. Your holding will claim income for what it earns from leases or real estate revenue. Keep proper records of these transactions! Activities are done through the operating company. Such activities include the sale of goods that produce revenue for the business. The benefit of this separation of activities is protection from creditors. Your holding company should never be conducting the same activities as your operating company.

The holding company's primary goal is to act as a lender or lessor to all the operating companies. As such, the holding company owns the assets, and your operating company leases them from the holding company. Remember, the trust owns 100% of the holding company. Our goal is to avoid taxes. Each operating company pays a lease expense to the holding company.

As an example of this tax avoidance strategy, the wealthy understand that the IRS will allow an LLC to 70% of its income towards a lease (yes, the same kind of lease the holding company will give you), so say, for instance, that you have sold your equipment, assets, real estate over to the trust and holding company. Now, you are leasing it back from them. We will make this simple for this example and use the trust and LLC's operating company. If $1,000,000 of income is produced by the operating company and you use the trust bank account to send 90% of the trust - $900,000. You are leaving $100,000 of taxable income with the LLC. But because you are leasing your equipment, land, etc., back from the trust, you can use the IRS tax deduction of 70% towards the $100,000 because of the leasing. $70,000 of that $100,000 goes back to the trust. Giving the trust a total of $970,000 now and the LLC with $30,000 of taxable income that you would have to report on your individual tax returns. However, you can use the standard deduction of $12,950 (2023 rate) towards the $30,000. Your taxable income is now reduced to $17,050 because of the standard deduction, with $970,000 going directly to the trust in a non-taxable event. A wealthy mindset allows you to understand this system of wealth that calls for tax avoidance, which is legal. When filing for taxes, you will file for the trust, holding, and operating companies separately. When you reach this level, find a good tax attorney that understands what you are doing. Turbo Tax can help you with these complex structures. Most importantly, keep all accounts separate and records on hand. You're building wealth by Mastering Money, so how you conduct business on this level must be done correctly to protect you. Pass down generational knowledge!

MASTERS OF MONEY

USING TAXES

Every day, you turn on the TV or radio or open up a conversation with someone, and people always bash the wealthy for having or building wealth. It's funny because it's a part of their agenda to keep you in poverty. If your focus is on hating or complaining about their wealth accumulation, you are in no position to change your mindset or be able to look at their success and ask the question: How did they do it? How can I learn their wealth secrets for my family? Look at yourself. These wealthy people understand how to build wealth, which is a learned behavior, so that means that you can learn it also. Intelligence isn't your high IQ; financial intelligence is looking at a set of facts based on knowledge of the subject matter and creating something different out of it using the same knowledge accessible to every other person. Basically, you create something different from your initial question of why. Or How? None of these wealthy people are more intelligent than you. They just have capitalized on the knowledge and information they can access.

One of the ways the wealthy have built a massive amount of their wealth is by thinking about the tax code and legally avoiding taxes. This is one of the most important examples of what was said previously. The IRS doesn't hide the tax code or publications that explain how to file taxes. You pay the highest taxes as an employee and consumer because you trade your time for money. Think of the tax code as an incentive to do business with the government. The wealthy don't work for the government as employees to get these tax benefits; they operate as entities (LLCs, Corporations, etc.) because the tax code deductions, credits, and loopholes reside in operating as an entity to receive them. So, the tax code is public information; start at irs.gov; who is an employee trading time for money and reads the tax codes to get these benefits? According to USA Today, the wealthy avoid paying taxes to the tune of $160 billion a year. We worry more about the wealthy paying their "fair share" instead of using financial intelligence to take the same tax code and get the same breaks in the tax code to avoid paying taxes. The way the wealthy do this is amazing. Some use foundations, trust, investments, gifting, etc.

Foundations: They get an immediate income tax deduction of 30% for their contributions. However, the law only requires foundations to distribute 5% each year for charitable purposes. That is 5% each year for charitable purposes. That 5% is calculated based on the previous year's assets; the first year requires no distribution. More importantly, foundations don't pay taxes; you have control over it, with the added bonus of using the rest of the 95% of the money to hire family members and pay generous salaries. Avoid capital gains tax because you can deduct the full fair market value of the stocks you contribute and not pay capital gains tax. Crazy, right? But legally, if the foundation sells, it only pays a 1.39% excise tax on the capital gains. Wow!

Trusts were explained in detail earlier, along with the benefits of tax deferral and control of assets.

Investments of the wealthy are always different than what ordinary people would do or have thought of doing. The wealthy have Mastered Money by turning a typical salary into an investment opportunity to defer taxes. Listen, 90% of citizens earn all of their income from "wages and salaries," and the wealthy earn income from investments. Even CEOs who run big companies work, but they get complex contracts that include deferred compensation from stock options or stocks, which are not taxed right away like a regular 9 to 5 worker. They turn a salary into an investment by doing this. Outside of their CEO job, all other income comes from interests, dividends, capital gain, and real estate, which offers even more tax benefits like depreciation, which get dedicated from federal income taxes. All these examples are how a CEO that runs a company, and is this an employee, uses the tax code to defer taxes because they know the IRS taxes "income," and w-2 workers get taxed first and higher, so they instead turn their job contract into an investment by taking a $1.00 annual salary but accept compensation in stock and stock options that can be deferred or eliminated altogether. Then, as mentioned previously, they truly Master Money because when they need to purchase anything or pay for something, they go to a bank and use the stock or stock options equity to get a loan against those assets, and again, because it's a loan, it's tax-free! Wake up! Don't allow your experiences growing up. In poverty, keep your mind stuck. My goal is to teach you how to Master Money.

Gifting has an annual tax exclusion of $17,000 per person for 2023. The lifetime gift tax exclusion for 2023 is $12.92 million (married #2584 million) but can rise depending on inflation. Look at the inflation rising today in 2023. You get the drift. The wealthy have always gifted people, which can be written off on taxes without problem.

Masters of Money use all aspects of wealth building based on experience to avoid taxes. Another way the wealthy utilize the tax code, which you can also use, happens when they live as an entity and take the following tax deductions. All these are in the context of having a business:

- The cost of rewriting a store building is deductible.
- The cost of a building you purchase can be depreciated.
- Payroll Tax – deductible
- FICA Tax – deductible
- City or state gross receipts tax – deductible
- State unemployment insurance – deductible
- Disability fund – deductible (most states)
- State income tax or state business franchise tax – deductible

- State, city, or local sales taxes you paid on business purchases – deductible
- Real estate tax or property tax on real estate owned by your business – deductible
- Tangible and intangible property tax – deductible
- Business vehicle registration tax-deductible
- Gasoline tax, depending on business mileage costs – deductible
- Telephone and cell phone tax – deductible
- Business travel – deductible
- Excise taxes are fuel taxes – deductible
- Items such as membership dues, stamps, safe deposit, box rental, and several others – deductible
- Tax penalties are not deductible, but interest charges on late payments are deductible for corporations only
- Fees charged to prepare your business taxes – deductible
- All business telephone services, fees, and taxes, either for landlines or cell phones, are –deductible
- Temp agency aid for finding employees for your company – deductible
- Tolls – vehicle tolls – deductible
- Tools – deductible (inexpensive with a life span of 1 year); expensive tools are depreciated over seven years
- Tractors and construction equipment can be deducted from the year of purchase or depreciated over seven years
- Trademark, meaning the cost of obtaining a trademark, service mark, trade name, or trade dress is amortized over 15 years
- Trailers/movable homes can be deducted from the year of purchase or depreciated over 5 years
- Travel by airplane, train, bus, or car – deductible
- Trucks can deduct the cost of using a truck for business
- Uncollectable accounts are deductible as bad debts, but only if they were previously in your income when the sale was made
- Vending machines can be deducted from the year of purchase or depreciated over seven years.
- Wages paid to employees of your small business are tax0deductible expenses if they are ordinary and necessary, reasonable in amount, and paid for services actually provided
- Warehouse renting is deductible

- Water and other utilities are deductible

- Website design is deductible

As noted previously, if you operate your life as an employee, you will never get to write off all of the above deductions. Tax deductions lower your taxable income, so the wealthy use it so effectively. A tax credit directly reduces your tax bill (ex., a tax credit of $1,000 will lower your taxes by $1,000). Other tax strategies that should be used to Master your Money are:

• Gift-Lease Back Technique

What if I told you that it was a way to deduct your asset twice? Let's use a car as an example, or you can use any other equipment used for your business. Once you depreciate that asset down to $0.00, which only means you took all the deductions you could get from it, you can gift it to someone in a lower tax bracket and lease it back from them.

Gift Asset $\Rightarrow$ Lease Back Asset $\Rightarrow$ You get the tax write-off for the lease expense $\Rightarrow$ Reduces taxes you pay $\Rightarrow$ They get the income

• The Augusta Rule

So, you can rent your house to your company up to 14 times per year without needing to report rental income on your tax returns—this applies to primary, secondary, and vacation homes.

One of the purposes of you understanding this now before you get home is so you can understand that going home to get a job is crazy if you have read all these four books. More importantly, with these taxes, the most important thing I will ever educate you about on this subject is this: "If you make money off the money, you don't pay taxes on it; but if you make money off work, you pay taxes."

Become a person who does the former, not the latter. The poor and middle-class pay taxes on what they make, while the Masters of Money only pay taxes on what they spend (e.g., on the Stock market).

Pro se Tip: (!)

Don't try to copy other successful people, to Master Money, understand why what they do works, then find new ways developed through action, to utilize new strategies in your life.

The most powerful code in the IRS that is used by the wealthy in business is IRS Code Section 162-A. What you can do with this code is amazing. It explains what a write-off is. After you read that, the three names that will stand out are:

- Reasonable

- Ordinary

- **N**ecessary

This is called the RON Rule; it means that if it's Reasonable, Ordinary, and Necessary in the pursuit of business income, it's a write-off. If you are paying for something that provides income for the business or is necessary for you to conduct business, then it's reasonable and can be written off.

Understanding this allows you to realize that as you live as an entity, you benefit from the tax code. When you don't live as an entity and don't understand the tax code, you are like the 71% of Americans who use services like Turbo Tax, etc., which are mostly automated and save time. Still, because you lack knowledge of the tax code, you force yourself to overpay in taxes.

To become a Master of Money, you must make sure that you understand that the wealthy don't pay taxes because their wealth comes from businesses, not from jobs. Ran as separate legal entities until themselves. They also don't take income or dividends from their businesses, which would create a taxable event. What they do instead is borrow against the value of their company. So, they have equity in the company that is worth a lot of money. Then, they use a big banking institution to get a loan against their equity shares, which is also tax-free because loans are debt, not income. Stay close. I am going somewhere with this. Usually, workers take income that's taxed first. The Masters of Money borrow against the equity, thus creating a "non-taxable event" because they are not getting income from their company. They are getting a tax-free loan from a bank against their ownership in the company. Then, they use that tax-free loan to buy assets that produce income to pay the loan back while gaining even more equity from another source to wash, rinse, and repeat. Ordinary citizens' #1 expense is taxes! Not for the wealth! They use trust, tax code, cash value life insurance, and businesses as tax shelters. As a Master of Money, you build up assets across sectors, then borrow against the value that wants to be built, creating debt that is completely tax-free. Change your mindset, change your bank account.

Another lesson that I can't begin to stress enough is that to create wealth, you have to create debt. Look at the top of any bill: $1.00 bill, $5.00 bill, $10.00 bill, $20.00 bill, $50.00 bill, $100.00 bill, and you will see that it says "NOTE" at the top of it, that's a real-life simple and easy way to show you that every one of them that's created and brought into existence is "debt". Yes, "notes" are debt! Understand it and use it to create wealth. Okay, let's move on to the next important tax loophole.

Section 168 allows for something called "cost segregation" with "accelerated appreciation," which allows commercial real estate owners to write off up to 40% of the property's value in year one of ownership. When you write something off, you are taking a loss against the actual income that you made.

> [For example, if you make $200k this year in profits, you can buy a building for $600k and take a $200k loss, and you'll pay zero $0.00 in taxes. Not only will you save on taxes, but you can also buy the building with O.P.M. – Other People's Money.]

Once you realize that taxes are for the poor and the middle class, when given the opportunity to purchase assets that produce income, they become consumers and buy a house to live in and cars to drive. See, the wealthy produce jobs for the economy. They also know that debt is tax-free, so they take out loans to buy assets and then write off the profit as an expense. Loans are tax-free! Financial knowledge allows the wealthy to understand that the system is set up to give money to the wealthy but has no way of getting it back from the rich.

Another tax resource the wealthy use is "depreciate property IRS Pub. 946". This would be a "non-cash loss." All this means is that the IRS lets you write off a big purchase for your business, like a rental property, even though it really didn't lose value.

Ex: Say you pay $215,000 for nine units. Now, you get a special evaluation done (wrote off $63,000 in losses). Take the property to the bank and say they add that depreciation back to the income because it's a "non-cash loss," so you can qualify for a loan, no problem. The appraisal comes in at $450,000; no upgrade done, and the bank hands you a check for $360,000 $\Rightarrow$ cash/check $\Rightarrow$ tax-free (it's debt now). With depreciation, you will save $25,000 on taxes, - $215,000 purchase = $170,000 gain. You got $170k to purchase this property. Now the $360,000 loan (mortgage) becomes a payment that your tenants will pay, and you will net $19,000 of cash flow a year! That is the power of the tax code and financial literacy, which gives you the knowledge you need to really understand the tax code so that you can take action.

Sitting in your prison cell gives you an advantage over 80% of Americans in society who are running the rat race, trading their time to be a worker instead of a person who controls assets. Your advantage is "time." How many people working up to 16 hours a day and 40 hours a week are reading the 6,000 pages on taxes? None, while they are continuing the cycle of financial slavery. But you have nothing but time on your hands. Take advantage of it. Check this out: of the 6,000 pages on taxes, only 40 pages are devoted to raising taxes. Read that again! So, you have the time to do just that: take a meaningful step towards managing your time.

If only 40 pages raise taxes, the other pages are meant to encourage you to do business in a certain way. Understanding these tax codes is your first lesson on building wealth. Time is your advantage! Most people don't know how to build wealth because there is an information gap between where they are and where they want to be. You never take the time to understand wealth, but you expect to get money without even knowing about money!

As a prisoner, we know better than anybody about what's referred to as the "system." What usually happens is that once we wake up as prisoners or average citizens in society living below the poverty line and start opposing the system, we are financially silenced by pressure from the system. The ones who succeed keep pressing on because you can't silence free financial knowledge. We can't expect things to get better by complaining about the system or how it's treating us while at the same time refusing to play the game of power, politics, and money. Imagine if you don't read about taxes that the wealthy use. You will forever be controlled by the people you hate.

To escape poverty, you have to see and take advantage of opportunity, which means taxes and the tax code are at the base or foundation of that.

Pro se Tip: (!)

20% Down Payment. You shouldn't put 20% down on real estate, because for every 10k you put down you will only lower your payment on average about $50.00 a month. This should only be done as a last resort. Get lower %'s.

Start with knowing what the tax code is! Which is just a set of laws and regulations that govern how individuals and businesses are taxed. It defines what type of income is taxable and what deductions can be taken. Although certain things change in the tax code, for the most part, the core of it has been the same. Because the wealthy either know or hire expert tax strategies, they take full advantage of the benefits and loopholes in the tax code. For the most part, the core of it has been the same. Because the wealthy either know or hire expert tax strategists, they take full advantage of the benefits and loopholes in the tax code. Speaking of tax loopholes, this is another way to avoid paying taxes legally. Tax loopholes are legal provisions in the tax code that allow individuals and businesses to reduce their taxable income and tax bill. One of the loopholes that are mostly used by the wealthy is the "carried interest loophole." This allows hedge fund managers and private equity managers (more on private equity in the next section) to pay taxes on their income at the capital gains rate, which is much lower than the ordinary income tax rate. Others include offshore, charitable donation, and depreciation loopholes – some mentioned.

You must take advantage of tax-free investments such as municipal bonds, which can reduce your otherwise taxable income. It's important to remember that tax loopholes are legal and are encouraged. To do this, you must operate as an entity in a structured eco-system where you control all assets but don't own them. There is so much power in knowing what the tax code provides because growing up with a poverty mindset made you believe the whole tax code and the IRS were out to get you. Poor financial literacy has allowed you to develop a scarcity mindset, complaining or hating people who have wealth because you don't have it. You get the same 2080 hours in the year the wealthy do, the same 40 hours in a week they get, so the one thing you don't complain about is the lack of financial literacy you have. Nor do you ask the question: How did they become wealthy? What are their strategies? How can I develop that wealthy mindset? How can I develop that wealthy mindset? You are taught to complain, not educate or question things. Taxes, to me, are great equalizers. They are the single most important financial area you should learn because wealth flows because of them, with such advantages as the cost of borrowing money, management costs, depreciation, and other allowable business costs. Always remember this: no matter how you think about the wealthy, no matter if the democrats tell you to vote for people who will increase taxes on the wealthy, it's all a system developed to help the business owner and wealthy. How are you going to tax the same people that create all the jobs? The wealthy will always find legal ways not to pay taxes. Those congressmen and women benefit from these same tax breaks the wealthy use.

This is why financial literacy is important, no matter your status, race, or gender. Once you obtain real financial literacy, which tells you how to build wealth using credit, LLCs, leveraging other people's money, etc., there are no more reasons to look at wealth as something that can only be obtained by a select few. Stop listening to broke people! The tax system shows you that employees don't get rich, but businesses do. So, create the business that creates the jobs. Rules are for poor people. So, you can only break the rules when you have the money to do so. One must understand the tax system and bend the rules to become wealthy. Stop moving slowly in your life and instead move with a sense of urgency. Coming from poverty, you must understand that you are operating within a closed system that rewards you for doing bad and takes those rewards away when you take small advancements towards financial freedom. That closed system is the welfare system, which pays people to fail. So, when they fail, they get the money. If they succeed at a minimum level, the money is taken away. This closed system makes people in poverty think that the purpose of money is to pay bills instead of learning such things as taxes that will allow you to build wealth and avoid paying bills. Understand the tax code!

MASTER OF MONEY

UNDERSTANDING PRIVATE EQUITY

Building wealth can be broken down into a lot of things. Many industries create wealthy people who run on million/billion-dollar systems, but they really don't compare to one category that has created more multi-billionaires than any other, and that's "Private Equity Investor" or "P.E." They buy deals off the market., you were probably thinking about real estate as the category that creates the most. If you really look at real estate in this present day, It has created 905 millionaires in the U.S., but it is the single least common way that people become on the Forbes 100 List. So yes, it created the most millionaires and fewest billionaires. Real estate has continued price compression, making investing in retail real estate much easier. This means more people are doing real estate, making it harder to build wealth. Access by more people equals price compression.

Pro se Tip: (!)

FIRMS

1. Vista Equity Partners – Robert Smith
2. Collab Capital – Jewel Barks Solomon
3. Harlem Capital – Henri Pierre – Jacque's
4. Backstage Capital – Arlan Hamilton
5. 645 Ventures – Aaron Holiday
6. Fairview Capital – Jo Ann Price
7. Base Ventures – Erik Moore

Private equity is a sort of alternative investment in which the investors purchase shares in privately held businesses. They look to take a controlling or substantial minority position in a company to maximize the value of that investment. Usually, the structures are as follows: **G.P.** General Partners.

L.P. Limited Partners

General partners are the "Firm," and limited partners are the "Investors". General partners and limited partners draft operating agreements which will establish "Target Returns," "investment Periods," and "Waterfall or Promote Schedule (profit distribution)." All this will be established through the "operating agreement". Now, general partners will have an investment thesis, track record, and their sourcing process to limited partners during the fundraising process. An example of how GPs and LPs make money is:

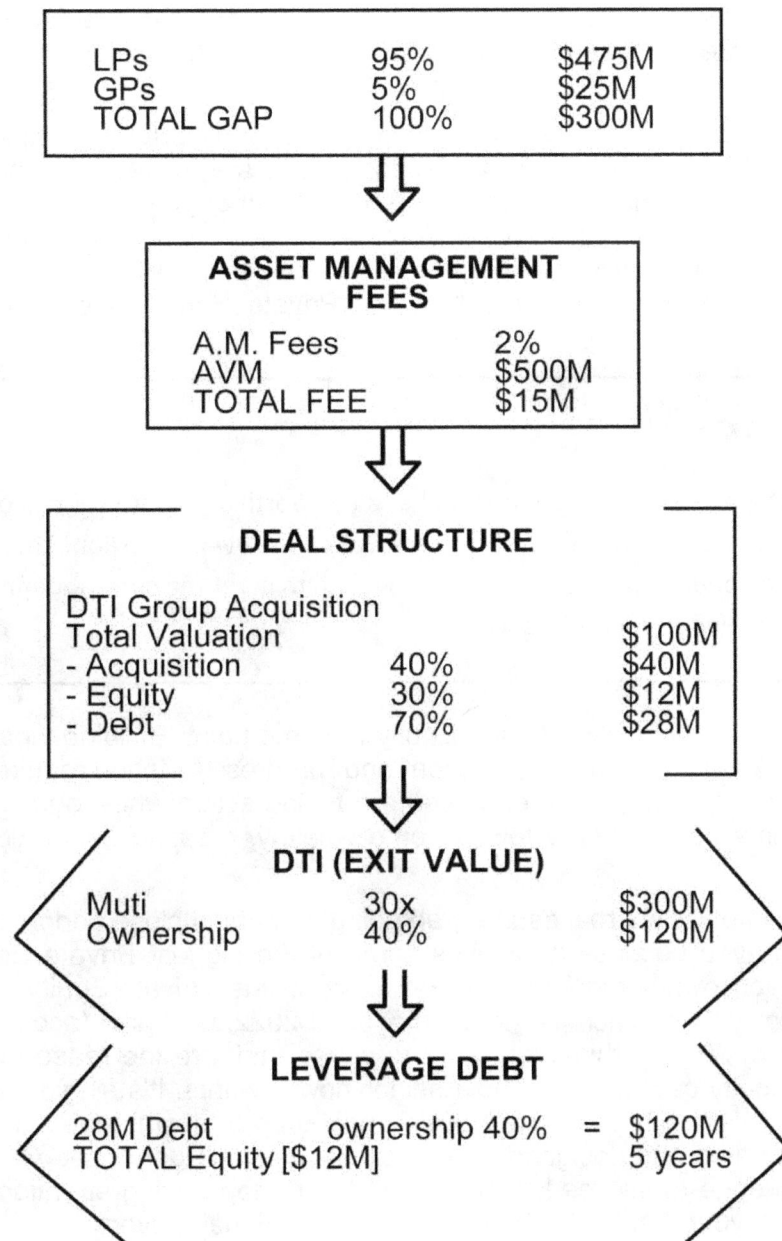

LPs	95%	$475M
GPs	5%	$25M
TOTAL GAP	100%	$300M

⇓

ASSET MANAGEMENT FEES

A.M. Fees	2%	
AVM	$500M	
TOTAL FEE	$15M	

⇓

DEAL STRUCTURE

DTI Group Acquisition
Total Valuation		$100M
- Acquisition	40%	$40M
- Equity	30%	$12M
- Debt	70%	$28M

⇓

DTI (EXIT VALUE)

Muti	30x	$300M
Ownership	40%	$120M

⇓

LEVERAGE DEBT

28M Debt	ownership 40%	=	$120M
TOTAL Equity [$12M]			5 years

This is a typical private equity deal structure that uses debt to leverage your position on the buyout.

A little history lesson: on or around 1946, two venture firms, 1) American Research and Development and 2) J.H. Whitney & Company, were a part of what was called back then "development capital" where only wealthy families and individuals could benefit from this type of Asset Management.

Of course, J.P. Morgan used private equity to manage the first leverage buyout of the "Carnegie Steel Company." Modern Private Equity is always credited to George Doriot, "The Father of Venture Capitalism." He also founded the American Research and Development Corporation, so the name is fitting.

The majority of these private equity owners make money by buying companies they believe have value and can be improved. All of these companies are "private" companies where P.E.s make money improving it, which will generate profits. Another way they make money is off the eventual sale of the improved company. Understanding this history will allow you to build your knowledge so you can eventually move to this field. Stephen Schwarzman became a billionaire by managing others' money and is the "King of Private Equity." He also co-founded "The Blackstone Group".

Pro se Tip: (!)

The top 2% of the United States population has a net worth of about $2.4 million. While the top 5% wealthiest American's have a net worth of just over $1 million. That means about 2% of the population possesses enough wealth to meet the current definition of being rich. (According to Yahoo Finance)

Creating your future has to involve Private Equity at some point. Building wealth and being rich are two different tasks. Just like having "motion" and "progress." Motion requires nothing but you to stand in place and job; progress means you are taking action while jogging down the street. Anybody can become rich, but very few become wealthy, creating generational wealth in the process.

Check this out; right now, it's a real estate grab going on behind closed doors that the traditional media isn't showing you because it involves some of the biggest Private Equity Firms in this Country, who probably own some form of these news outlets. Private Equity owns an estimated $239,018 single-family homes across the country as of 2022, until now (according to Americans for Financial Reform). Why is this important? Because they are the reason why the rents are going up! Private equity can move a whole sector how it wants. It's single-family homes today and tech tomorrow. Also, they can push housing prices up or down if they control the property. This system was created and designed in a certain way. Don't get upset. Get active. Now that you have the knowledge to succeed, then act on it and stop paying attention to these leaders who offer you and your family section 8 and generational poverty, with a side of mass incarceration. No financial book on the market will give you this in a four-book series designed to make you wealthy.

Ask around, wherever you are, and see if you can find five people who know what private equity is or how it works. Buying stocks is easy; put in $50-$100 a month or every other month in the S&P 500 Index, and you can build up a nice nest egg while sitting in a cell doing time for 5-10 years. However, private equity allows you to build wealth with a clear strategy in a specific sector. We are here to create Billionaires and wealth-building strategies that will allow you to build up generational wealth. While nothing about Private Equity is easy, everything is achievable.

Pro se Tip: (!)

Top Private Equity Firms

1. The BlackRock Group, Inc.
   $941 Billion (Assets under management)
2. KKR & Co. Inc
   $479 Billion (Asset under management)
3. The Carlyle Group, Inc.
   $376 Billion (Asset under management)
4. CVC Capital Partners
   $127 Billion (Asset under management)

Eventually, you will be at this point, so I didn't get into a lot here because I'm writing another book about this type of wealth-building later. But because you made it to book four of this series, you should have plans written down about how you will eventually achieve success by following the steps outlined in these books. Private Equity is where you want to be at the end of your journey. Above are the steps to achieve that; although short, it's concise and straight to the point.

Private equity has also outperformed the U.S. market over the last couple of decades. So, use the road map above to understand and carve out your plan.

HOUSE HACKING TIPS

1. Even if you start out as a 9-to-5 employee and start to build up a 401 (K), you can use your 401 (K) to lower your debt-to-income ratio so that you can qualify for a larger house. So, instead of paying interest to the bank, you're paying it back to your 401 (K), and if used correctly, it can really benefit you down the road. Using all sources of income available to offset something while gaining tax-free money is the key to mastering money.

2. Using a "Bank Statement Loan" allows you to get a mortgage without showing your tax returns or income documents, as most conventional loans are based upon. All you need is 12 months' bank statements; that house you want is yours.

3. First-time Home Buyers programs exist all around this country, but there is a program called "DPA Advantage," which works as a Down Payment Assistance Program. It gives you about 35% off of the purchase price as a grant. You don't have to pay that back. That's not even the best part; this program allows you to receive up to 6% in seller credits, which means you can ask the seller to contribute up to 6% of the purchase price to cover closing costs as well. Now, you will also be able to save on the upfront fees as well. An example of this process is as follows:

    Step One: Get the DPA Advantage Application and fill it out.

    Step Two: Go out and find a seller. Instead of getting a price reduction of 6% upfront on the price, get that 6% reduction as a seller concession to help you with your closing costs. So, what this means is that if you are buying $500,000, that 3.5% grant will cover $17,500, and that 6% seller concession will give you $30,000 to cover those upfront closing costs. Added together, that's approximately $47,500. Now that means you saved some money to put towards renovations.

Remember, you may read this and ask how I can do it. But the purpose might not be to do this right now; maybe you have family outside who could really utilize this. Masters of Money is about a mindset shift in financial knowledge. You understand how the wealthy used these strategies to build wealth. These books are your classroom and window into a world of wealth you have been trained to and taught to despise.

4. Another hack that allows you to gain access to homeownership is if you get 2 to 3 friends together and buy a $500,000 property. Next, you would write up a "Cohabitation Agreement" and a "Property Agreement" first. If all of you put up about $7,000 each into that property, that would be approximately a 4%-5% down payment on that $500,000

property. Each of you would own a piece of the property. You would also have to select who would live in the property for the required minimum of 12 months. After that, you can get a tenant there to pay the mortgage. You all would average a 5% rate of appreciation, which approximately gets you to 640K in just five years. Just on that one investment of $7,000, each of you could be sitting on $50,000 in equity once you sell.

5. Another house hack tip requires only that you ask one question; based on it, you can save thousands on your payment. The question is: "If the seller is on an FHA Mortgage," this needs to be asked to the listing agent. If they are on FHA Mortgage, it's great news for you. It means you can assume their loan. Essentially, they are transferring their moorage in your name. This will help you lock in a lower interest rate, typically 3%; these rates are generally high because of rising rate increases by the Federal Reserve. Right now, rates for mortgages are around 5%, assuming a potential FHA Mortgage at 3.0% saves you 3.5% and thousands of dollars.

6. Don't ever put 20% down on a property! This hack is more of a tip/warning. Don't listen to these people in books and on TV who tell you this is the right course of action. Look at this:

Example: 1) 600K Home 20% down = 120K After two years value dropped by 20% The new value is 480K	2) 600K Home 5% down = 30K
-120,000 cash Banks are more likely to foreclose on buyers who are 20% down.	-30,000 cash Risk on the bank & not the buyer

Just because you put 20% down doesn't amount to anything but a risk, and there is only a potential savings of $50 on payments. It also forces you to put in more money than you need to.

7. Down payment towards equity account. For first-time homebuyers, $25,000 is devoted to a down payment, which will transfer into equity in your home. Plus, the bonus is that you never have to pay it back.

TAXES OF THE WEALTHY
UPDATED

Always remember, the government is doing business with you and your company. The faster you realize that, the faster you can build wealth. However, the IRS has a special secret about this that they don't want citizens to know. And that's because you are a partner with the government. The problem lies in the fact that when you are a "W-2" employee, the government becomes the "Active Partner," and because of that fact, the IRS doesn't want you to become the "Active Partner." A lot of you all sitting in a cell, thinking about being a partner with the government makes your skin crawl because you have a "Poverty Street Mindset" It's funny because when I originally told someone about this, their mind went straight to some crazy crap about telling. LOL! We have to be better and change that mindset. Now, the IRS doesn't want you to know this because when you are the "Active Partner," you make the decisions, you pay less in taxes, provide affordable housing which gives you access to special tax credits, you are providing a service or good, and if you're that "Active Partner," you have the ultimate control over that money. That means tax credits & deductions, which ultimately allow you to be taxed on less money or not taxed at all because there is no income to tax.

Pro se Tip: (!)

With S-Corp tax status 20% of your net income is tax-free.
With Depreciation, you can only depreciate structures not land.

People have tried to figure out why the wealthy don't pay taxes. It's not that complex. They use debt, and they keep money moving through investment. Reinvested money doesn't get taxed. Another thing to know is that everything you use should be owned by a business, which allows you to harness the power of deducting everything. Most wealthy people use foundations to hide wealth because charity donations are not taxed. You can literally donate money, land, cars, etc., to the foundation. CEOs like Elon Musk and Meta's Mark Zuckerberg don't get a salary from the companies they run; if they do, it's $1.00. They take equity instead of a salary, like 95% of Americans do. Why? It isn't taxable unless you sell it. So, Elon Musk bought Twitter (now named X) for approximately $40 billion. He went to a bank and got a loan against the equity he owns, which is another tax-free event on his part because debt is tax-free, and a loan is a debt. Why do you think the wealthy own so much artwork? Because buying art counts as an expense and can be deducted. All you have to do is make the expense match the income in a business, and nothing can be taxed.

Wealthy people also give out gifts in the form of money. Right now, the IRS allows a cap of $15,000, with a lifetime cap of $11.7 million. Make sure each financial/money gift is under the $15K cap because it becomes a non-taxable event, plus it allows you to gift $11.7 million over that person's lifetime.

Another example of the wealthy's taxes is when they borrow against business assets, which means they are not required to pay taxes on money from banks or lenders. The business and its assets are used as collateral.

There is a misunderstanding in the real estate investment world, where citizens believe they need to be a realtor or hire a realtor to sell real estate, purchase real estate, or even conduct business in the real estate profession. Why would I be bringing this up in a tax section? Well, at some point, 99.9% of all things financial or investment-wise lead you straight to the IRS and its tax codes, straight to the IRS and its tax codes. Wealthy people who deal in real estate know that the IRS doesn't care about you being a realtor; as long as you pay them, you can do a lot in this market. According to the IRS, you don't need a license to be considered or qualified to be a real estate professional and reap the benefits of this. Only two points need to be met. 1) Need to spend 750 hours engaged in the business of real estate; 2) More than 50% of your business activity also has to be in real estate. The benefits lie in the tax code itself. You can write off real estate depreciation towards your active income. That means if you're making a lot of money on something outside of real estate, you can start writing off that income with real estate, as long as you qualify as a real estate professional, by using the above two IRS qualifications. Dedicate half your work week toward real estate. While you make your income working or somewhere else, you are able to get the deductions from buying rental properties to offset it.

- Cost segregation studies are common practices to offset active and passive income. You can even show a loss using this wealthy tax strategy. Cost segregation goes as follows: buy a rental property, write off everything that's on the inside of the property (i.e., appliances, bathroom, etc.) When you write everything off that's inside the property, it creates a big expense (cost segregation study). Once this is conducted, it will create a big enough loss to offset W-2, 1099, stock, and crypto income, making you tax-free. With W-2 employees, you will still use the previously talked about real estate professional qualification or make the average stay in your rental property seven days or less. By chance, if you do create a loss, it's in the "depreciation bucket," so when you go to the bank, you didn't show 70K; you showed the government 70K. With the bank, you showed them 100K because it's depreciation. It's the only line item on tax returns you can add to your income and losses. Many people call this the "paperless strategy." Most of your family right now in the outside work as W-2 employees or 1099 contractors. They can offset that income by utilizing the above strategy, thus starting the wealth-building journey. Now, if you plan on going home and getting a job, this is a good way to offset that income.

- Moving on, DSCR Loans are really good. No income, tax, or employment verification is required. Important here is that you don't need tax returns from the IRS to qualify. The deal qualifies if the rental income exceeds the monthly payment. Even if the property is vacant, it's okay because they (banks) will use an "estimated market rent" to qualify.

- A lot of people with mortgages try to pay them off quickly, but another tax benefit is to keep it for as long as possible. Why? Let's say a rental property is $250K. 1) You must consider the opportunity cost; with real estate, you can bring a fraction of the money, and banks will lend the rest. Then, purchase another property that gives you a higher return. 2) Tax Advantages: Mortgage interest is tax-deductible; bonus depreciation 3) Harvest Equity and purchase more cash flow-producing assets. So, keeping mortgages longer helps you benefit from taxes.

- Trading Stocks for everyday people creates a lot of tax problems because they are uneducated about the IRS codes and what's allowed when investing in the stock market. Think beyond the stocks themselves and look at the advantages of the tax code and its benefits to you. When buying and selling stocks, you get hit with short-term capital gains taxes. One thing you could do is create an LLC. LLCs are just entities you can use to trade stocks under instead of your name. This allows you to write off different things that will help you offset potential gains. Some of these things include Anything used for trading, such as (monitors, laptops, screens, etc., and any type of trading subscriptions you have; tools, flow services, and even mentorships are all write-offs, helping your taxable income. Live through your LLC, not as an individual.

- Crazy as it sounds, planes are 100% tax write-offs for new and used planes. If used for business purposes in the first year, it can be used as a 100% tax write-off immediately after purchase. The first year for business and 50% for business in the second year. Fly like the 1% of wealthy people.

  For example, $1 million in taxable income - $1 million in plane deduction = $0.00 in tax bills.

- S-Corp tax status is another tool of the wealthy. Let's just say that you have the following:
  $125,000 Revenue
  $ 25,000 Expenses
  $100,000 Profit

Salary still must pay F.I.C.A. taxes (40%   60%) Distribution No F.I.C.A. Taxes

40K.	X	15.3%	=. $6,120
60K	X	0.0%.	= $0
100K	X	15.0%.	= $15,000
		TOTAL =	$21,000

S-Corps allows you to avoid double taxation. S-Corps pays no Federal taxes. Earnings and losses are passed through to the owner. Dividend distributions are free of FICA taxes (Medicare and Social Security). S-Corp allows you also to be an employee of the business and draw wages as employees. LLCs taxed as S-Corps are best, especially when used in conjunction with a holding company LLC.

- 8 Real Estate Tax Advantages that can also help you. Depreciation (non-cash expenses) deduction from income. This real estate tax deduction is based on the perceived decrease in the value of the real estate. Mortgage interest tax deduction from income, the interest you took for your mortgage loan. Deferral of capital gains via 1031 exchange cost of repairs, maintenance, and upkeep; cost of services (rental property management and legal consultation or service); utilities; travel cost associated with the property (checking on the property inspection, repairs, etc.); property tax deduction.

- Low-income housing tax created developers. Previously, I spoke about the Government, and you are going into business as the "active partner." By using Section 42 of the IRS code, which is the low-income housing tax credit section, you become an "active partner" with the government. There is a crisis with affordable housing in this country right now, so you use this to your advantage and become wealthy in the process. You can essentially syndicate the credits that the state gives you. Put in an application, and they say okay and approve the application. Next, they award you credits, and you can take those credits and get them syndicated. This means only that you go to a company and say I got these $500,000 worth of credits, and the tax credits are a 10-year award, so that's $5,000,000. They say I will buy it for $0.43 in the dollar. Then you get $4.3 million in equity to go and build it; that's where equity rolls in. Include L.I.H.T.C., which means landlords get to claim tax credits for eligible buildings in return for renting some or all of the units to low-income residents with restricted rents. Provide services the government needs, and you will become wealthy, understanding the tax code is an incentive-based system that rewards "active partners" and not W-2 employees.

Pro se Tip: (!)

The IRS helps you pay mortgage payments when you buy a primary residence the interest paid each month is tax deductible against your "Annual Income."

EXAMPLE

Tax Rate	Interest	Balance	Monthly Payments
24%	$1,860	$495,339	$2,533 ⇓ Reduces to $2,000

By applying this mortgage deduction, you save $445/month.

Remember that the income tax code is approximately 180 years old. Multiple changes have occurred, but the framework that was established back then still exists. Using it to build wealth is and should be the only thing on your mind. Taxes make the wealthy wealthier and make the poor poorer. The only thing that separates you from the wealthy is your mindset and your financial knowledge. This is your crash course in financial education that a lot of you weren't taught in school. Use this to help your family and you build wealth. Study and take action on your plans. The tax code is an inventive based system that makes you an "active partner" with the government, doing the business the government requires to keep society running (affordable housing), the best time to get loans and tax credits to build affordable housing for people, is right now because the government is in a crisis to provide affordable housing. Look at the system and follow the trends. It will lead you to wealth creation. Take a look at the tax code and use it as a roadmap to buried treasures.

People think that all they have to do is work hard and keep their heads down, get a 401(k), and retire, and that's a way to achieve success. Now, think of the guy working hard to make French fries at McDonald's. He is sweating over that grease but doesn't have the success level he dreams of having. It's crazy! You have all the time right now in prison to set yourself up nicely before you go home, which leads me to say you must maximize every second of your time. All these strategies will still work if you are never getting out of prison. Some men and women in prison aren't going home – that's the reality. You can still build wealth to live well there, but more importantly, you can help your family and friends on the outside to set the family up and create generational wealth based on what you know. That's you leaving a legacy. Use the tax code to achieve this.

Pro se Tip: (!)

We get so caught up on a couple dollars that we are scared to imagine obtaining a $100,000 or even millions of dollars. Take for instance that if you make $274 a day X 365 days = $100,000. Only $274 a day will get you $100,000 a year. You can make it happen.

Wealthy people use taxes to build wealth; they aren't focused on a Forbes 100 list of billionaires and who got the most money. Their net worth is something you care about; 100% of the time, it's not accurate anyway. Let's just say, for instance, that you have a $2 million net worth, but it's tied to your personal residence, cars, and boat. This means that you would have to leave your big house and earn more money to pay for that $2 million net worth. It's laughable how here in prison, we get Forbes or watch TV shows about business or stories about the richest person in the world, and we get caught up and distracted by that B.S. Remember, that list is smoke and mirrors, Elon Musk or whoever Forbes list isn't the Richest in the world. People like the Suadi Royal Family members are never listed in Forbes, nor are the leaders of O.P.E.C., etc. They are worth trillions, not billions.

Let's get back to our story and look at how the wealthy look at net worth or lack thereof. Say you have the same $2 million net worth, but instead of being tied to personal residence, boats, etc., you have it tied to investments. Making $50,000 to $100,000 a month means you have the knowledge to deploy that money while you sleep to make money. So, you don't have to worry about net worth. You focus on your investment portfolio worth. Look at the median net worth and income charts combined to show you each class breakdown and why they make you think the secret 1% level is hard to reach, but it's really not.

MEDIAN NET WORTH   **MEDIAN INCOME**

MEDIAN NET WORTH	Class	MEDIAN INCOME
$608,900	Upper	$187,000
$201,800	Upper Middle	$125,000
$104,700	Middle	$71,000
$43,760	Lower Middle	$48,500
$6,030	Lower	$27,000

CLASSES (U.S. CENSUS)

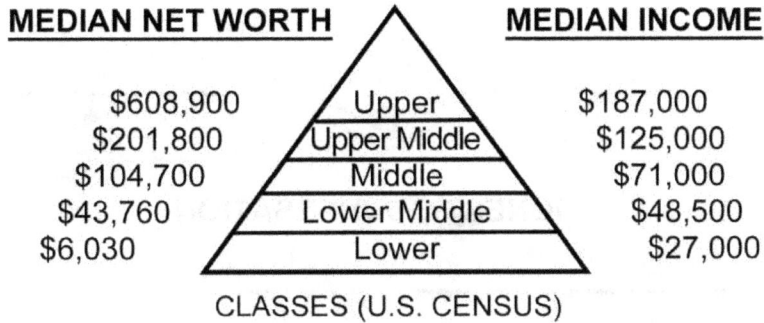

Nothing you learned in school, from the hood, or wherever before you picked up these books will have given you this knowledge. Understanding taxes and using debt will take you further in your financial quest for financial knowledge.

HONEST CONVERSATION

Don't get caught up in the cycle of prison. Once, I lost myself, and there were no direction and financial obligations facing me. Hard choices needed to be made, so I studied the finances of the wealthy. Long story short, I got it together and learned that poverty was created for a reason, but I learned how to get out and do a lot with little; we should stop trying to blame wealth and study it. Take their information and use it for yourself. They don't hide it. The problem I've seen and heard is that no one has taught like I taught them about wealth in such little time with such clarity. What I have found out through my research about prisoners and also the formerly incarcerated is that they want to learn finances, business structuring, etc., but don't have a person with similar circumstances teach them. We all learn in different ways, which is fine, but to hear this knowledge from someone like you in a prison cell hits differently. It's like you in a prison cell hit differently. It's that feeling of if he can do it, then so can we. That's what this whole "Pro se Prisoner" brand is about: a resource for the incarcerated to build wealth, devise a plan, and execute it without risking their life and coming back to prison. Standing in a corner watching for robbers, police, and potential sales is hard. Risking your life to pull a trigger because you hustle on one corner, and someone sold on your corner and you told him not to is hard. We claim blocks we don't own any real estate on, have no stores on, or own no tangible things around there but the clothes on our backs. We hustle on blocks our family is renting on. That's why you run when the police come; no homeowner is running off their porch because of the police presence, and that ownership of real estate comes with constitutional protections.

So, I said all that to have a real honest conversation about taking that same gangster bull crap living you slaved on a corner living, and turning that energy into building an LLC, buying real estate, obtaining credit, fixing your credit, or building your credit. The ultimate goal is completely removing yourself from poverty and developing a wealthy mindset. After studying about building wealth, the one thing that stuck with me the most was a saying: "Become intentional with your actions." That quote has become my life motto, my words to live by. Make sure every action you take is intentional. From the time you wake up till the time you go to sleep, take every step to live with your plans, but make sure the actions you take are intentional, with no second guessing. The most successful people are long-term thinkers.

Create your own wealth formula that allows you to consider what you've learned here. So, let me give you the one I created for myself almost 8-9 years ago.

Pro se Tip: (!)   WEALTH FORMULA
C.A. KNUCKLES

1. Learn about How to Build Wealth
2. Learn How to Make Money
3. Learn How to Protect Money from Taxes
4. Learn How to Make it Grow
5. Build Generational Wealth

Building wealth is a slow process. It's up to you to realize that at the point you are ready to hear it. Prisoners sit in prison and read "Rich Dad, Poor Dad" and study it and think that's the wealth formula, but when I first read that book, I had limited financial knowledge; ten years later, I've learned to build real Wealth from real wealth builders, and there are so many holes in that book that you wouldn't know because you haven't walked the wealth path. Just read my four books and tell me if that other book gives you the real building wealth strategies you need to succeed now and when you return to society. Why spoon-feed you like a baby? Giving all the knowledge allows you to make the decision on what path you want to take on your journey instead of directing you to one path. No one is you, and that is your power. The system has a mindset that says: "Never educate a person you are going to dominate." That's why financial literacy isn't taught in the schools you attended; it's not taught in prison, either.

In prison, I see untapped potential in everyone inside these restricted walls. Even the worst prisoner has something to offer. Society can learn so much from prisoners, but society doesn't want to. That's why I created "Pro se Prisoner" to cultivate that potential. I refused to sit around and wait for a corrupt system to help. Pro se Prisoner steps in Pro se Prisoner is owned by my other company below:

The Attic Group, LLC
1 E. Chase St., Ste. 1101
Baltimore, MD 21202

You can write to that address and request the business information you need, which you can't get yourself. Remember, we are building a Prisoner Virtual Assistance business where you can write and get things done that you need. Also, check out our website (www.theatticgroup.org). Click on the "Pro se Prisoner" tab. That's for the people who can get their contact people to help them. But for those who can't, just write to the address above for assistance.

Oh yeah, my last book, Pro se Prisoner: How to Buy Stocks and Bitcoin, came out in 2021; there have been complaints about not getting the DRIP stock applications from companies. Technology has changed things, and most of these companies have developed an online portal that you have to go to their stock agent to get. So, if you go to the above website (which is mine), it's a section with all the companies on there. Fill out the form and list the company name you want for the application, and it will be sent to you. You can also write the above address, request the application for any company, and request the DRIP list with all the companies. Yes, it's a minor thing for me, but I know it's big for you, so I developed our own Pro Se Prisoner portal to obtain these lists and applications for our community. Thanks for understanding.

$\Diamond S \Diamond$

CONTINUED EDUCATION

Building wealth first starts with changing your mindset. Mindset is everything; you must shift your thinking. We were programmed to be poor and not to understand basic personal financial principles of money. Also, you'll need to rethink the working hard mindset; it's a myth that if you work hard, you will build wealth. That's what the wealthy tell you: so that you can keep the lights on and keep your mindset locked in on a goal of working hard for them while you never go anywhere. Held within this book are the building blocks of wealth. It teaches you not to work harder but smarter. Your problem in prison is knowledge, or lack thereof, not time. You are positioned in prison right now to have success at all costs because you control time and have more of it than the average person in society. Knowledge of these books will solve problem #1.

Recently, I've seen and recognized that people who grow up in poverty with a poverty mindset don't reach financial freedom or are held back because they always defer back to who and what came before them. It's up to you to change that financial path of poverty that has come down from generations before you. It's not just a knowledge gap for some; you have to believe you can build wealth. That's why I write as the Pro se Prisoner to show you what's possible from prison. What I write, I have done. Listen, it's about time you read this, and I get a thought, idea, or action off my chest on these pages. I've moved on to the next stage of financial growth. Again, I will take action and repeat this to you and give you the knowledge. Right now, I'm caught up on my financial history. Who controls what? How are they building wealth? Who is behind the curtain of these financial falls in our society so we can learn and use them to build up our communities and families? Financial history is important because it shows the promise and effects on impoverished people. It's going to change what you think you know about money. Get out of your own way and believe in yourself.

Changing your mindset requires you to stop looking at success and successful people and hate or envy them. Look at their success and learn how they did it while also realizing that you have the same 24 hours in a day to achieve whatever you want. Remember, your advantage is sitting in a cell with all that time. I provide the knowledge you research and develop a plan to take action. The #1 Secret to Success is "Time"; effectively use yours. Recognize the power of the time that you have sitting in that cell. Becoming a Master of Money has more to do with understanding "time" and "mindset" than purchasing things. Assets are important, but knowing myself and changing your mindset first elevates you faster.

Understand this: The wealthy know that the purpose of money is to buy time! Yes, that sounds crazy, but that's the wealth system. You have to be talked about as crazy because when you ascend beyond society's known data point about someone who grew up with a poverty mindset,

I would look at you like you're crazy because you weren't supposed to make it out, but you did.

Pro se Tip: (!)

You must reduce your burn rate. The rate at which your burning cash. Salaried workers with access to money increase their burn rate. The more money they make the more they burn. Wealthy people, buy time, so rather than spending money they keep it because they understand it buys them time.

-Vusi Thembekwayo

Once the mindset is reprogrammed, you can focus on building up your assets to take your financial state to the next level. Wealth is accumulated through mindset change, the accumulation of assets and resources that can be used to produce income and provide financial stability for generation after generation.

Wealth is a slow process, while wealth is first mixed with hard work and having one or two of a high income or significant amount of money. People who are looking from the outside believe that every person with millions of dollars, nice cars, and big houses makes them wealthy. No! These rich people are just that rich! They are not wealthy because if their high income isn't accompanied by substantial assets/ownership, they are just rich.

Some wealth-building steps you can take on your continued educational journey are:

- Access to assets that are generating cash
- Use liquidity to generate new forms of liquidity
- Free cash flow generating assets
- Appreciation and capital gains
- Diversification and risk management
- Leverage and borrowing power
- Intergenerational wealth transfer

Other examples used have been talked about previously, but just to touch back on it briefly. The Rockefellers, yes, hate them or love them. They have generational wealth lessons we can learn from. That formerly had one question for lawyers and their financial advisors:

> "What can we do to utilize the law to separate and protect our wealth from exposure to estate taxation?"

After much debate, they came back with the idea to "utilize a trust," specifically on "irrevocable trust" that can't be changed once declared. Stop! Using the above method, you should already produce income and have several assets. Now, you will start aggregating a certain portion of your wealth and pushing it over to the trust. These trusts have their own tax ID number, are separate from you, and their own entity, own tax schedule, pay taxes, and file tax returns. Once assets are transferred, there is nothing to tax at the estate level. Rockefellers leveraged trust vehicle to shift wealth to trust. What they understood and you can take lessons from this, was that if you could shield a portion of your wealth from taxation generation after generation, you could create a perpetual wealth vehicle for generations as they have.

Your whole life is built around taxes. Just try to look at it this way:

- Earned Money = Income Tax

- Spend Money = Sales Tax

- Buy, Create Value, Then Sell = Capital Gains Tax

- DIE = Estate Tax/Inheritance Tax

Studying what the Rockefellers did allows you to utilize their strategies to create massive opportunities for you and your family. But your goal should always be to pay less taxes utilizing the trust structure because taxes are on erosion of wealth. For all the negative people reading this thinking, I'm in prison. I can't do this, or uptown (home) thinking it. Both of you can do it, as long as you are producing income, which by book 4, you should already be in phase 2 or 3 if you have support out there to put this in place. This process is as simple as this:

- Having disposable income

- Set up Irrevocable Trust

- Set up earlier, like at birth for kids or now for kids and adults in your family.

- Buy life insurance for each member of the family.

- The trust will be the beneficiary of these cash value policies.

Instead of complaining or giving up, leverage this financial knowledge to learn how to leverage assets and then build wealth for every generation after yours. Instead of this old saga of working hard for your entire life, thinking you will be successful, change your mindset, and move with intention and a sense of urgency. Although you work hard, what you want in life changes to move with a sense of urgency.

Masters of Money require more than regular tactics deployed by the average 9-5 hustle of life. Wealthy people become connoisseurs of information and ideas. Poor people look for information and ideas that confirm what they already believe. The former understands the game is to use that information to build wealth. While the latter don't play the game of wealth but instead take the short road to justify what they already know. But don't get it misunderstood. The wealthy deal with mindset adjustments, too. Getting wealthy and staying wealthy requires different mindsets. These are real battles that cause problems for wealthy people.

Pro se Tip: (!)

"Idealistic people are controlled by Pragmatic ones. You have no power because you are willing to give it up."

-Unknown

During this continued education, remember that most of everything contained in these pages consists of how to obtain wealth—at the same time, showing you the roadblocks and miseducation of the poor. Rules are in place for the poor. So, you will only be able to break these rules when you have the knowledge and money to do so; after that, you will succeed in life at whatever you want. In this current financial system, that's not changing at the present moment; the people who do hard work rarely get rich. The employees don't get rich. The businesses do. Investors rarely get rich. The patent owner does. Entrepreneurs make money, but the venture capitalists you went to for money make more by doing less. Find your position and add value because it produces value (economically).

Sitting in that corrupt environment, don't forget that over 90% of you grew up in impoverished ghettos, living by some code that you were told was the best thing that happened to you. Open your eyes to those who want to keep you poor; do so by convincing you and your family that wealth and the financial system are complex. I wrote this book series to show you that it's not; you were just blocked from knowledge. Once you have that, it's easy to understand because you just have to act on your plan. Utilize your tools to control the system: Debt and taxes! Leverage to build wealth for multiple generations.

Recently, I came across an interesting fact and data point that should put this whole Guide to Build Wealth series into perspective. There are approximately 330 million people in the U.S.A.; there are only approximately 788 billionaires out of that 330 million! Read that again! Understand that this wealth-building process is serious, and if you want to build wealth for generations, then numbers like the ones above should generate drive and eagerness to succeed. Working hard is the myth to keep you in poverty, with dreams in your head about what could have happened in your life. Working smart and calculated is the road to wealth. Wealth is quiet and slow. By all means, financial slavery exists; drawing up plans to keep people impoverished and depending on the government or business owner for a job is real. Control the flow of money, and why should I care about your laws?

My personal motto is "I woke up this morning; everything after that is a choice I make." Most people ask people in prison how they're doing today, and that's always my answer—no matter who asks the question. First, I can't control if I wake up after sleep. On a side note, I don't sleep a lot. I have been up late, like 5:00 a.m. or later, taken a 15-minute nap, gone to my medication after breakfast, and been awake all day, wiring and learning. Second, once I'm up, no correctional officer, warden, or prisoner can make choices for me because how I respond to anything is my choice; how I talk to you is my choice; how I move is my choice. No one controls that but you. Remember that. Each choice you make on this financial journey is yours compared to finance and wealth building. If you want to be average and sit on your ass and not succeed, that's your choice! Bold leaders are the ones who make a difference. Time is something you or nobody can manufacture; everyone has a finite, limited amount of it. Take note of your choices because time can't be manufactured.

Your education never stops. It continues in this process of building wealth. Success takes time! Thinking creates the most wealth because you are utilizing your brain. Opposite to wealth building is labor, which creates the least amount because you are trained to think you're only supposed to make money based on your labor. I'm going to give you a quick example based on research I have been doing for my next book: Pro se Prisoner: Financial History. Our grandparents, parents, uncles, and aunts were taught for multiple generations to work hard, save money, and put money into your 401(k) so that when you retire, you will be set for life. You would be able to live calmly and travel around the world. Sounds like an "ad" from some financial institution. Looking at history, the 401(k) scam placed on our family member then when it was created is still here today, tricking our generation with the same bull crap. Let's say you got $500,000 dollars in your 401(k). My question to you is, "How much of it is yours?" Your answer: "All of it, I saved it or rather put it in my plan every paycheck." The reality is that it's not all your money; once you entered into the 401(k) scam, you became a "limited partner," and the federal government became the "general partner" of your plan. This allows the government to tax money from you without knowing how much and at what point it goes up or down. Right now, that percentage is between 38%-39%. That means 38%-39% of your plan is given to the government. But what happens when that 38A% goes up to 50%-60% or 70%? History has shown us that it was up to 90% in the past! Can you imagine living in the 1950s, giving your labor away, and 90% going to the government in the form of taxes? In the 1950's, the marginal tax rate was 90%. This one example shows you that hard work and giving labor don't make you successful. Your labor doesn't determine success; the wealthy know how not to pay taxes and know never to use 401(k) plans because they have read the 5,000 plus pages of the tax code or paid someone to do it for them, thus buying time. Great leaders hire around their weaknesses.

Many of us like to look at ourselves as hustlers and be active in the game. Our involvement in the game is like a badge of honor and respect for impoverished ghettos. What if you kill the "hustler"? Outside those neighborhoods, are you successful? In that prison cell, after everybody left you, are you still a hustler? Kill the Hustler! What got you to this point of picking up these books is in direct conflict with what will allow you to read these books and allow them to show you how to build a wealthy mindset. Wealthy mindsets know that you have to deactivate that hustler side that's telling you to do everything and be 100% active. Being CEO and building wealth doesn't require you to be a hustler, so leave it at the door before you walk through this wealth-building door. Don't bring an oppressed mind into a financially free construct.

Sometimes, this requires you to think outside the box, as billionaires do every day. People think that we are not in a recession, but the Fed has yet to get inflation under control. Opportunities arise in these environments we're in now. Follow me through a financial history lesson. In the 1973 Bear Market and 1981 Bear Market, the wealthy invested in fine art, which beat inflation. Contemporary art is appreciated by 33% annually, which means it outpaced GOLD and REITS equities in that same period. Why? Art is an "asset" that is not linked to the performance of stocks. Today, it's the same thing. You can see these opportunities if you have changed your mindset. Morgan Stanley's research found that art sells 24%-26% more at auction than last year. That's real gains, not that poverty mindset of 401(k) and savings accounts at banks that lend 90% of your money to wealthy individuals for pennies on the dollar. Wake up! But most of us don't have millions around to really make massive gains. But there is always a solution to problems. Stop speaking about the problem and instead ask yourself, "How do I find a solution?" A " Masterworks " platform allows you to invest in shares of multi-million-dollar art instead of owning it. Starting small is fine; you have obtained the knowledge now, so all that's left is to execute at your own pace. Because all money comes into circulation as debt, which devalues currency already in circulation as debt, which devalues currency already in circulation, your labor is always being affected by this current state of money. On the other hand, the wealthy use business and tax deductions instead of labor because you can get a 30%-40% tax deduction for every dollar you spend on business expenses. Change your mindset! The wealthy don't talk about labor, they're taking their money investing in companies that are about to thrive and just sit back and collect money. Remember, in this book, I told you that private equity creates 95% of all billionaires; millionaires are made in real estate. Investing in these companies is a form of private equity. Stop trading your time for money. Basically, who you are or were raised now needs to be set free and let go. Don't let the memories of your past be stronger than the vision of the future you wish to create.

CONCLUSION

So, we are at the end of a groundbreaking book series, Pro Se Prisoner: Guide to Build Wealth. Let's end where we started. With a question:

What are your core values?

1. _____
2. _____
3. _____

Now, look back at the start of this book, where you had to answer the same question. Look at what changed based on your knowledge of the book series you just read. Give three new core values now, and watch the mindset shift from the earlier answers. Becoming a Pro se Prisoner Master of Money requires your core values to change because you can't be the same person you were in the beginning that you are now that you read this book series on building wealth. Operate from the perspective and not your perception. Simply put, wealth secrets aren't in a hidden vault, underground, guarded by a secret organization. Yes, powerful people and organizations can move whole economies, but each started by understanding how to build wealth and the language of money. 1 in 10 people die wealthy. Most people die broke and young (U.S. Census). Set goals for six months that you would have set for two years out. This simple modification will force risk.

The craziest thing I heard, but the most important thing I learned while researching for these books, is behind the curtain: "Information." Have it. You succeed; don't have it, fail or are limited by the little you know. Information is key because you can then execute it. Utilize properly designed structures and leverage vehicles to keep building wealth. Sitting in prison, we seem to lose hope fast. It's a moment in time we all go through. These books are meant to show you that you can be successful in prison. As a prisoner myself, I've accomplished a lot. I own over 150 stocks that I've had since 2010, and I own multiple LLCs that generate income – year over year—cryptocurrency, real estate, transportation business, publishing, etc. Nothing is off limits; never limit yourself because you are in there. Yes, most people don't have people on the outside to help them. Get started (my company is working on that now to provide financial services, bank accounts, and investment opportunities directly to you – Including assistants). Many times, our families don't know how to help us because they lack financial literacy, so it's up to you to share this knowledge with them. Your plans and execution should be the same. Teach them to help you; help them. Somebody said, "You attract the frequency at which you resonate." What you do or push out into the world is what you get back. Previously, I told you that while in prison, I plan for my departure by studying and learning what's important to succeed. Your greatest asset is the time you have to study and learn. Use your disadvantage of being in prison with limited resources as your advantage to take action.

Now, you have the formula to build wealth without limits. No more complaining; you are now only in a position to offer solutions. Confidence comes from action, so take action in your future and stop waiting for others to do it for you. Masters of Money are not entrepreneurs; they stop starting businesses from scratch and graduate to buying existing businesses with cash flow, using other people's money (private equity). Just as there are steps in a house, your prison unit, etc., that lead to the next level, that's the same as building wealth; it's multiple levels. So, the question to ask yourself is, why not you? You have the knowledge and the plan; take action now. Stop operating and thinking for a sense of lack, a fear of not having enough, and/or a belief that success is reserved for a privileged few. Develop a wealth mindset where you are willing to take risks and achieve them, giving you access to financial success.

A prison cell is whatever you want it to be; I've decided whatever you want it to be; I've decided to make it into my business office. Really, you have the power to turn yours into anything you want it to be, just don't waste time on bullshit! Your mindset is critical to your financial success and fulfillment in life. Adopting a wealthy mindset and making shifts will unlock your full potential of becoming a Master of Money. This series was meant to delve into the intricate world of finances, but from a building wealth perspective, which usually involves demystified and complex concepts. I broke those concepts down from these books so you can see that it's really not that complex once you get into it. Use these books to pave your way for a brighter future.

For more financial news and financial booklets, go to my website theatticgroup.org.

REWARD:
ADDITIONAL RESOURCES

- Debit vs. Credit
- Business Credit Cards
- 150 Banks for Business
- Vehicle Financing Lenders
- 26 U.S. Code § 7702 – Life Insurance Contract Defined
- 15 U.S. Code § 1681(b) – Permissible Purposes of Consumer Reports
- 15 U.S. Code § 1681(c) Requirements on Info in Consumer Reports

• DEBIT VS. CREDIT

Many people around the world choose to use banks as a way to hold their money. There are large national banks as well as smaller local banks. One of the main benefits to using a bank is the convenience of not having to carry cash with you. It is also a good way to track your spending thanks to online banking websites and apps. Those who have a bank account, will usually open both a checking account and a savings account.

A **checking account** is considered your main account. It is a place where you put most of your money or funds. You can choose to have your paychecks sent to your bank automatically though **direct deposit** or you can take cash directly to an ATM or bank teller and have it put into your account. Checking accounts are used to make purchases and pay bills. They also come with a **debit card**. A debit card is a plastic card that can be used online and in stores to make a purchase without carrying coins and cash. In order to use a debit card, the user will have to set up a **PIN** number. A PIN number is usually a four digit number that has to be entered for each purchase in order for the card to work. It helps protect against theft and fraud. That way, if you loose your card and someone else finds it, they won't be able to use it unless they know your specific PIN number. Many account holders also receive **checks**, which is another way to pay or send money to a person or company. When the person or company receives your check, they can deposit that amount into their own bank account.

A **savings account** is similar to a checking account, but it is not used for spending. It is a place where you can put money to save it for later. Some people have savings accounts for **short term goals**, like saving for a vacation or a new car. Others may open a savings account for **long term goals**, like saving for retirement or an emergency. Savings accounts usually allow you to make money off **interest**, which means the more money you save, the more money your bank will add to your account. Sometimes your bank may give you an ATM or debit card for your savings accounts, but they will usually limit the amount of times your can take money out. Remember, the goal of a savings account is to see how much money you can put into it, not how much you can spend.

Credit cards are much different than debit cards. When you use a credit card, you are borrowing money that isn't yours with the promise to pay it back. You are given a **credit limit**, which is a set amount of money on your card that you can borrow. You will get a statement, or bill, each month with the option to make a **minimum payment** or to pay off what you borrowed in full. Credit cards can be helpful when you need to make a purchase, but do not have enough in your checking or savings account to pay for it. However, you have to be very careful. Unlike checking and savings accounts where you can *make* extra money through interest, with a credit card, you will have to pay extra in **interest fees**.

Credit card holders also have the convenience of not having to carry cash and are usually better protected against theft and fraud since the money is owned by the bank. A lot of credit card companies also offer **rewards** to their cards, such as cash back or points. For example, if your credit card company offers 5% cash back, that means every time you spend $100 they will give you $5 back. Credit cards also help build your credit history and if used responsibly, can improve your credit score. A **credit score** is a number between 300-850 that is used to represent how responsible you are with finances and how likely you are to pay bills on time. Having a good credit score will allow you to have higher credit limits. It also provides you with more options if you choose to get a loan for a larger purchase, like buying a house or car. The higher your score, the less risk you are to the banks.

PARTS OF A CARD

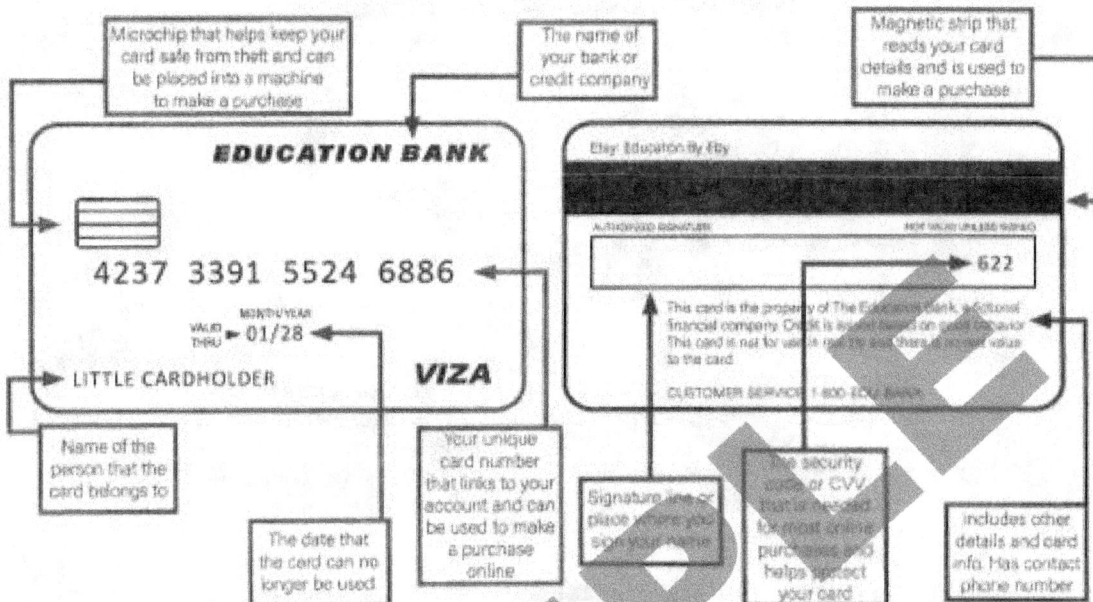

Microchip that helps keep your card safe from theft and can be placed into a machine to make a purchase

The name of your bank or credit company

Magnetic strip that reads your card details and is used to make a purchase

EDUCATION BANK

4237 3391 5524 6886

MONTH/YEAR
VALID THRU ▶ 01/28

LITTLE CARDHOLDER

VIZA

Etsy: Education By Etsy

AUTHORIZED SIGNATURE   NOT VALID UNLESS SIGNED

622

This card is the property of The Education Bank, a fictional financial company. Credit is issued based on good behavior. This card is not for use in real life and there is no real value to the card.

CUSTOMER SERVICE: 1-800-EDU-BANK

Name of the person that the card belongs to

The date that the card can no longer be used

Your unique card number that links to your account and can be used to make a purchase online

Signature line or place where you sign your name

The security code or CVV that is needed for most online purchases and helps protect your card

Includes other details and card info. Has contact phone number

DIRECTIONS: Print out this page. Then cut out the front and backs of the debit and credit cards below. Color them and sign your name on the signature line. Place the blank sides of the front and back of the cards together and laminate for more durability if using for pretend play.

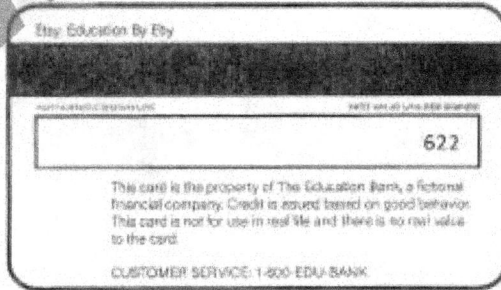

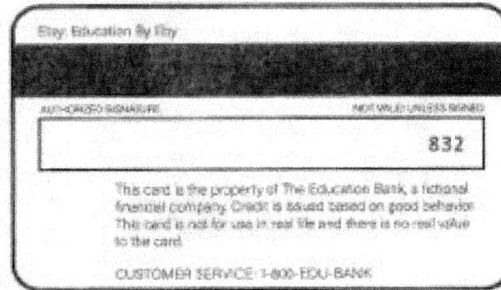

EDUCATION BANK

4237 3391 5524 6886

MONTH/YEAR
VALID THRU ▶ 01/28

LITTLE CARDHOLDER

VIZA

Etsy: Education By Etsy

AUTHORIZED SIGNATURE   NOT VALID UNLESS SIGNED

622

This card is the property of The Education Bank, a fictional financial company. Credit is issued based on good behavior. This card is not for use in real life and there is no real value to the card.

CUSTOMER SERVICE: 1-800-EDU-BANK

EDUCATION CREDIT

9987 6544 3211 0099

MONTH/YEAR
VALID THRU ▶ 07/28

LITTLE CARDHOLDER

Etsy: Education By Etsy

AUTHORIZED SIGNATURE   NOT VALID UNLESS SIGNED

832

This card is the property of The Education Bank, a fictional financial company. Credit is issued based on good behavior. This card is not for use in real life and there is no real value to the card.

CUSTOMER SERVICE: 1-800-EDU-BANK

PARTS OF A CHECK

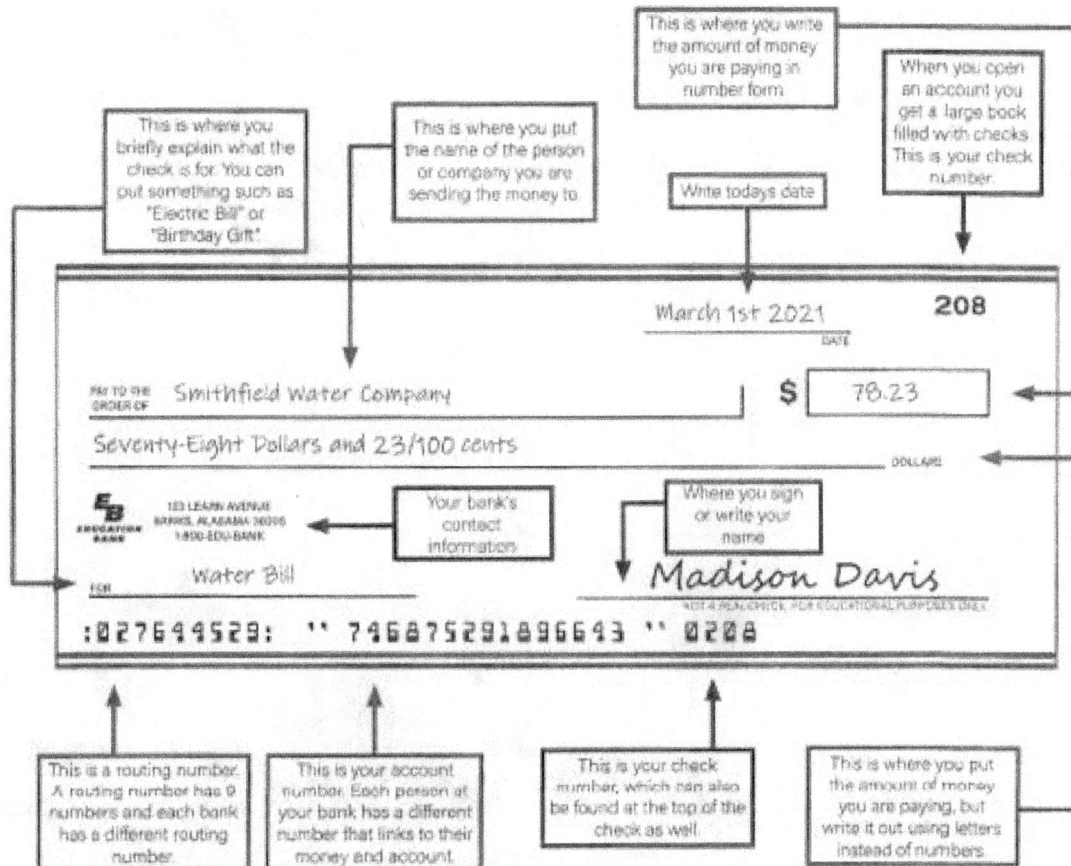

This is where you briefly explain what the check is for. You can put something such as "Electric Bill" or "Birthday Gift"

This is where you put the name of the person or company you are sending the money to.

This is where you write the amount of money you are paying in number form

When you open an account you get a large book filled with checks. This is your check number.

Write todays date

March 1st 2021   **208**
DATE

PAY TO THE ORDER OF   Smithfield Water Company $ 78.23

Seventy-Eight Dollars and 23/100 cents   DOLLARS

EDUCATION BANK   123 LEARN AVENUE
BANKS, ALABAMA 36000
1-800-EDU-BANK

Your bank's contact information

Where you sign or write your name

FOR   Water Bill   Madison Davis
NOT A REAL CHECK, FOR EDUCATIONAL PURPOSES ONLY

:027644529:   '' 746875291896643 ''   0208

This is a routing number. A routing number has 9 numbers and each bank has a different routing number.

This is your account number. Each person at your bank has a different number that links to their money and account.

This is your check number, which can also be found at the top of the check as well.

This is where you put the amount of money you are paying, but write it out using letters instead of numbers.

DIRECTIONS: Print out the blank checks on the following page. Practice writing checks for different amounts.

OPTIONAL: Cut out and laminate the checks. Use dry erase markers to write the checks so that they can be wiped down and reused multiple times.

INTEREST

WHAT IS INTEREST? When you use a credit card you are using borrowed money. Why do banks want you to borrow money? So they can make money off interest. If you do not pay back the money you borrowed in full, then you will be charged an interest fee. Most credit card interest fees, also known as the APR, is usually around 15-27 percent. The longer it takes you to pay back the money, the more money you will pay in interest over time.

There are different types of interest: Fixed, Variable, Simple, Compound and Prime. Each method can be calculated differently. For this lesson we are going to focus on simple interest.

DIRECTIONS: Read the questions below and calculate the amount of interest that would be charged for each purchase. Then calculate the total cost of the item.

Dashawn buys a plane ticket to Montana. The plane ticket costs $382. His interest is 15% which is equal to $57. If he agrees to pay back the money within 2 years, how much will the ticket really cost?

	$57	YEARLY INTEREST	
x	2	NUMBER OF YEARS IT TAKES TO PAYOFF	
	$114	TOTAL INTEREST	

$382 COST OF ITEM
+ 114 TOTAL INTEREST
$496 TOTAL COST

Mariana wants to pay for her college tuition. The tuition costs $4,697 for the year. Her interest is 8% which is equal to $375.76. If she agrees to pay back the money within 5 years, how much will the tuition really cost?

YEARLY INTEREST

X   NUMBER OF YEARS
           IT TAKES TO PAYOFF

_____   TOTAL INTEREST

COST OF ITEM

+   TOTAL INTEREST

_____   TOTAL COST

Olivia wants to pay for a new guitar. The guitar costs $1,999. Her interest is 28% which is equal to $559.72. If she agrees to pay back the money within 1 year, how much will the guitar really cost?

YEARLY INTEREST

X   NUMBER OF YEARS
           IT TAKES TO PAYOFF

_____   TOTAL INTEREST

COST OF ITEM

+   TOTAL INTEREST

_____   TOTAL COST

INTEREST

Fatima wants to buy a new car. The car costs $16,500. Her interest is 12% which is equal to $1980. If she agrees to pay back the money within 3 years, how much will the car really cost?

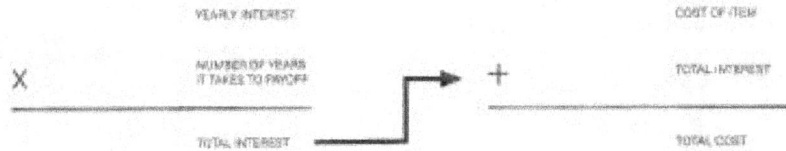

YEARLY INTEREST		COST OF ITEM
X NUMBER OF YEARS IT TAKES TO PAYOFF	→ +	TOTAL INTEREST
TOTAL INTEREST		TOTAL COST

Chen wants to go on a cruise. The cruise costs $600. His interest is 3% which is equal to $18. If he agrees to pay back the money within 8 years, how much will the cruise really cost?

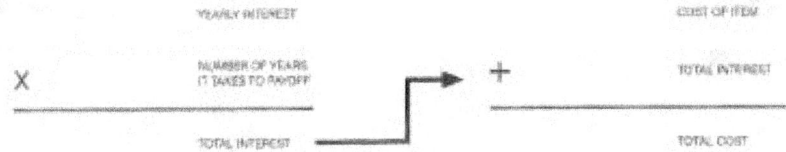

YEARLY INTEREST		COST OF ITEM
X NUMBER OF YEARS IT TAKES TO PAYOFF	→ +	TOTAL INTEREST
TOTAL INTEREST		TOTAL COST

David wants to buy a gift. The gift costs $175.99. His interest is 17% which is equal to $29.92. If he agrees to pay back the money within 1 year, how much will the gift really cost?

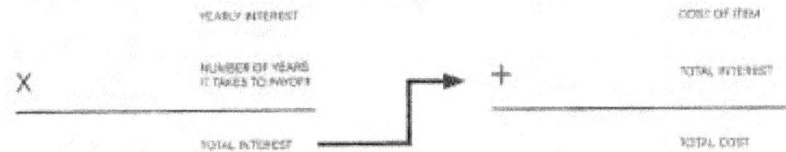

YEARLY INTEREST		COST OF ITEM
X NUMBER OF YEARS IT TAKES TO PAYOFF	→ +	TOTAL INTEREST
TOTAL INTEREST		TOTAL COST

Tyrell wants to buy a wedding ring. The ring costs $3,200. His interest is 5% which is equal to $160. If he agrees to pay back the money within 8 years, how much will the ring really cost?

YEARLY INTEREST		COST OF ITEM
X NUMBER OF YEARS IT TAKES TO PAYOFF	→ +	TOTAL INTEREST
TOTAL INTEREST		TOTAL COST

OVERDRAFT FEE

WHAT IS AN OVERDRAFT FEE? When you use a checking or debit account, you use your own money that you currently have in the bank. If you try to make a purchase and you don't have enough in your account you may get a decline, which means you will not be able to buy the item. However, in some situations, the purchase may go through even though you don't have enough money in your account. When that happens your bank may charge you an extra fee called and overdraft fee. An overdraft fee can be $20, $30 or another amount the bank chooses. It is a good idea to budget and keep a record of your spending so that you do not have to pay extra fees.

DIRECTIONS: Read the questions below and decide if there is enough money in your account to cover the purchase without being charged an overdraft fee. Circle your answer.

YES / NO There is $259.55 in your checking account. You need to pay your car payment, which is $309.22. Do you have enough money in your account to cover the cost without getting charged an overdraft fee?

YES / NO There is $952.47 in your checking account. You need to pay your rent, which is $800. Do you have enough money in your account to cover the cost without getting charged an overdraft fee?

YES / NO There is $350.11 in your checking account. You need to pay for groceries, which is $145.34. Do you have enough money in your account to cover the cost without getting charged an overdraft fee?

YES / NO There is $50.67 in your checking account. You need to pay for gas which is $20. Do you have enough money in your account to cover the cost without getting charged an overdraft fee?

YES / NO There is $517.19 in your checking account. You need to pay your electric bill, which is $213.99. Do you have enough money in your account to cover the cost without getting charged an overdraft fee?

YES / NO There is $400.01 in your checking account. You need to pay for a hotel stay, which is $609.55. Do you have enough money in your account to cover the cost without getting charged an overdraft fee?

YES / NO There is $163.28 in your checking account. You need to pay your phone bill which is $163.78. Do you have enough money in your account to cover the cost without getting charged an overdraft fee?

YES / NO There is $12.75 in your checking account. You need to pay for lunch, which is $8.99. Do you have enough money in your account to cover the cost without getting charged an overdraft fee?

READING A STATEMENT

WHAT IS A STATEMENT? A statement is a monthly document that shows important information about your credit card or bank account. On a credit card statement you can see your interest charges, due date, minimum payment, rewards, balance, credit limit and APR. Bank account statements show your deposits (money you put into your account), transfers, interest earned, routing and account number and any overdraft fees. Both credit and debit accounts show your transactions for that month and any terms and conditions. It is a good idea to look over your monthly statements to make sure all the charges are correct and there are no fraudulent charges.

DIRECTIONS: Use the printed credit card statement to answer the questions. Then fill out a blank check for at LEAST the minimum amount due.

What is the last 4 digits of the card number? _____

When is the payment due by? _____

What is the minimum payment due? _____

What will happen if you make a payment on June 6th at 9:00pm?

_____

How much rewards cash is available? _____

Why was there no interest charged on the last statement?

_____

What is the previous balance? _____

What is the credit limit? _____

How much credit is available to spend? _____

How much was spent at WaWa Gas Station? _____

When did the Home Depot charge post? _____

Whats is the APR? _____

Where can you go manage the account? _____

Based on the information given, when would be a good day to send in your payment by mail?

_____

How much does Education Credit charge for a late fee? _____

What is the current balance? _____

EC EDUCATION CREDIT

Page 1 / 2
Education Credit Card | card ending in 0099
Apr 12, 2021 - May 12, 2021 | 31 days in billing cycle

Payment Information

Payment Due Date	**Jun 06, 2021**

Balance	Minimum Payment
$2,011.80	**$46.00**

If we do not receive your minimum payment by 8:00pm on the due date there is a late fee of $40.00

Rewards Summary

Rewards Balance	$75.36

Rewards can be redeemed for checks, gift cards and account credits. Go online for more details.

Account Summary

Previous Balance	$1,006.99
Payments	- $1,006.99
Transactions	+ $2,011.80
Cash Advance	+ $0.00
Fees Charges	+ $0.00
Interest Charged	+ $0.00
New Balance	**= $2,011.80**
Credit Limit	$4,500.00
Available Credit	$ 2,488.20

Transactions

LITTLE CARDHOLDER #0099

Transaction Date	Post Date	Description	Amount
Apr 17	Apr 19	Home Depot #2256	$1,675.23
Apr 27	Apr 28	Walmart #3478	$297.65
May 2	May 5	WaWa Gas Station #1119	$38.92
Total Transactions			**$2,011.80**

Interested Charged

Interest charge on purchases (last statement)	$0.00
Interest charge on cash advances	$0.00
Total Interest	**$0.00**

Your APR is 20.99% for purchases

- -

Pay or manage your account at www.educationbank.com

Customer Service 1-800-EDU-BANK

Payment Due Date: Jun 06, 2021

New Balance	Minimum Payment	Amount Enclosed
$2011.80	$46.00	$ _____

Please send this part of your statement along with a check to Education Credit. To ensure your payment is received on time allow at least 7 days for delivery.

EC EDUCATION CREDIT

Send Payments To:
Education Credit
123 LEARN AVENUE
BANKS, ALABAMA 36005

VEN DIAGRAM

DIRECTIONS: Use the ven diagram to compare and contrast both credit cards and debit cards. Use the information that you have learned in this lesson to help you. Cut out the statements below and paste them in the correct part of the circle. Can you think of any other similarities or differences that are not mentioned? If so, simply write them inside the circle.

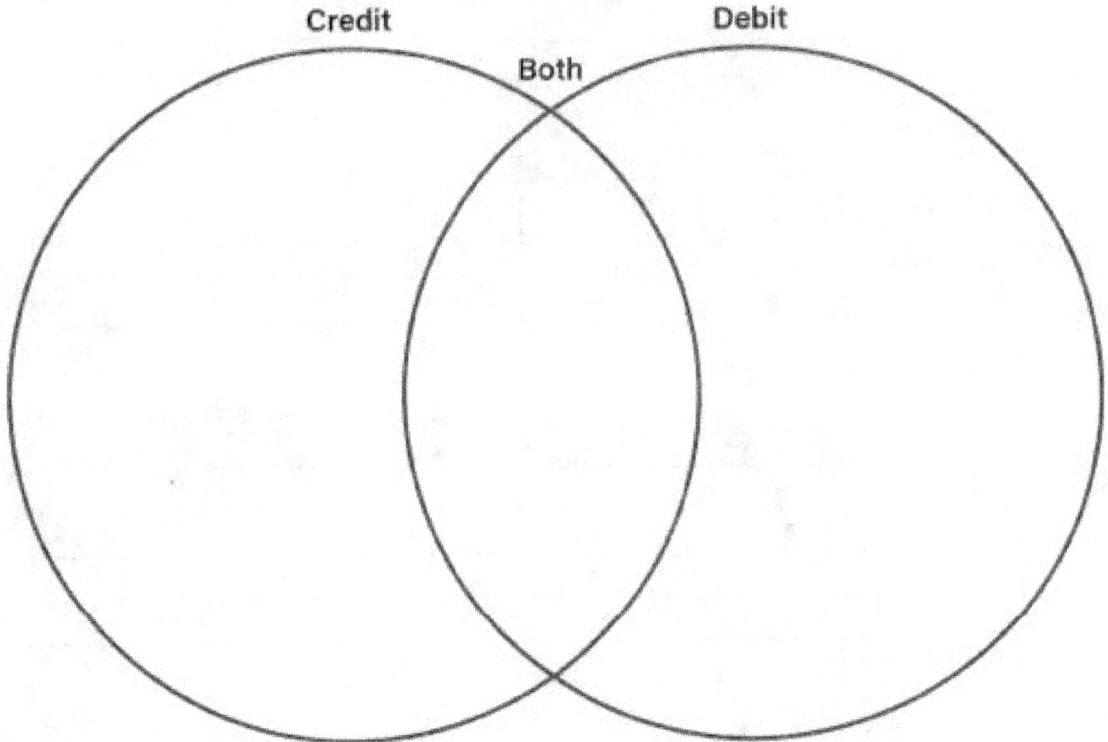

Credit   Debit

Both

borrowed money	requires a pin number	uses money that you currently have
makes interest	can offer rewards or perks	charges interest
provides a monthly statement	can charge overdraft fees	provides a physical card to use in stores
requires a minimum payment	links to a checking or savings account	helps build credit history

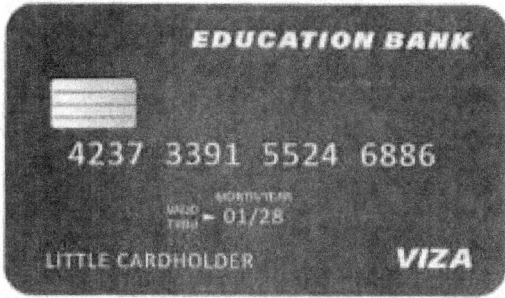
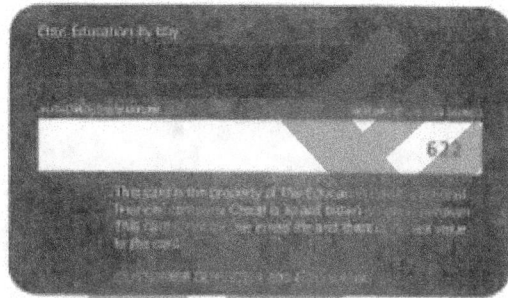

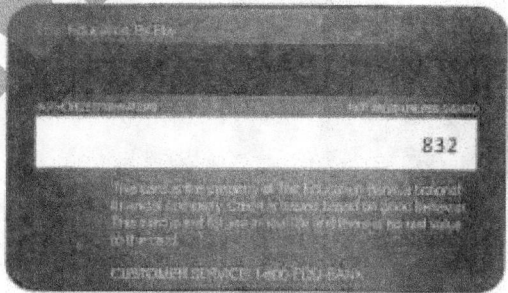

• BUSINESS CREDIT CARDS

Business credit cards can offer several benefits to businesses of all sizes. Some of the key benefits include:

Improved cash flow management: With a business credit card, you can make purchases for your business without tying up your cash reserves. This can help you better manage your cash flow and ensure that you have enough funds to cover unexpected expenses.

Before you apply for business credit cards, make sure your personal credit profile looks something like this:

- FICO scores of at least 680
- 2 or more credit cards from major banks
- Cards must be 2 years old
- $2500 limit minimum
- Usage under 35%
- No late payments in 24 months
- No bankruptcies
- No charge off
- No collections

• Chase Ink Business Cash

- 680 Fico score
- 1 year in business
- Pulls from Experian

• American Express

- 680 Fico score
- 1 year in business
- Pulls from Experian

- ## **Truist Business Cash Rewards Credit Card**

- 700 Fico score
- 1 year in business
- EIN needed

- ## **TD Bank**

- Reports to Experian and Equifax
- Revolving terms
- EIN needed
- D&B number needed
- 2 years in business
- Do not put in an SSN, but call and ask for a manual review if the above qualifications are met; if you put in an SSN, they may make a personal inquiry

- ## **First National Bank**

- Reports to Dun and Bradstreet and Experian
- Net 30, 60, and revolving terms
- EIN needed
- D&B number needed
- If social is required on the application, ask the credit department if credit will be pulled or if it is just for informational purposes

- ## **PNC Cash Rewards® Visa Signature® Business Credit Card**

- 670 Fico scores
- EIN needed
- 1 year in business
- Pulls from Experian

- **Citizen Bank**

- 680 Fico score or higher
- 0% APR for 6 months
- Need EIN
- Soft pull from Equifax

- **KeyBank**

- Soft pull from Equifax
- Revolving terms
- 15% interest rate
- No annual fee

- **Home Depot Commercial Revolving Charge Card**

- 2 years in business
- Established business credit report with Experian
- Revolving terms
- May PG
- Low monthly payments

- **Lowe's Business Advantage**

- Must PG
- 2 years in business
- EIN needed
- 0% Interest for 60 days
- Revolving terms

- **Corpay Mastercard**

- Good to excellent credit
- 90 days in business
- Personal credit score of 680
- $50,000 annual revenue

• **BANKS**

- JP Morgan Chase

    https://www.jpmorganchase.com

- Bank of America

    https://www.bankofamerica.com/

- Wells Fargo

    https://www.wellsfargo.com

- Citibank

    https://online.citi.com/US/login.do

- U.S. Bank

    https://www.usbank.com

- PNC Bank

    https://www.pnc.com/en/personal-banking.html

- Capital One

    http://www.capitalone.com

- TD Bank

    https://www.td.com/us/en/personal-banking

- BB&T

    https://www.bbt.com

- Sun Trust

    https://www.suntust.com

- Regions Bank

    https://www.regions.com

- Fifth Third Bank

    https://www.53.com/content/fifth-third/en.html

- M&T Bank

    https://www3.mtb.com/personal-banking

- Huntington Bank

    https://www.huntington.com/

- Santander Bank

    https://www.santanderbank.com

- KeyBank

  https://www.key.com/personal/index.jsp

- BBVA Compass

  https://www.bbvacompass.com/

- Discover Bank

  https://www.discover.com/online-banking/

- Ally Bank

  https://www.ally.com/

- American Express Bank

  https://www.americanexpress.com/

- Barclays Bank

  https://www.barclaysus.com/

- BMO Harris Bank:

  https://www.bmoharris.com/main/personal

- Charles Schwab Bank

  https://www.schwab.com/bank

- Chase Private Client

  https://www.chase.com/personal/private-client

- CIT Bank

  https://www.cit.com/cit-bank/

- Commerce Bank

  https://www.commercebank.com/

- First Citizens Bank

  https://www.firstcitizens.com/

- Flagstar Bank

  https://www.flagstar.com

- HSBC Bank

  https://www.us.hsbc.com/

- Key Private Bank

  https://www.key.com/kpb/index.jsp

- M&T Securities

  https://www3.mtb.com/personal-bankingg/investments-and-insurance/inversting/m-t-securities

- Merrill Lynch

  https://www.ml.com

- Navy Federal Credit Union

  https://www.navyfederal.org/

- Northern Trust

  http://www.northerntrust.com

- People's United Bank

  http://www.peoples.com/personal

- Rabobank

  https://www.rabobank.com

- Raymond James

  https://www.raymondjames.com/

- Sterling National Bank

  http://www.snb.com

- Synovus Bank

  https://www.synovus.com/

- TIAA Bank

  https://www.tiaabank.com/

- Union Bank

  https://www.unionbank.com

- Webster Bank

  https://public.websteronline.com/personal

- Wilmington Trust

  https://www.wilmingtontrust.com

- Wintrust Bank

  https://www.wintrust.com/

- Zions Bank

  https://www.zionsbank.com

- American Savings Bank

  https://www.asbhawaii.com

- Arvest Bank

  https://www.arvest.com

- Associated Bank

  https://www.associatedbank.com

- Axos Bank

  https://www.axosbank.com

- BancorpSouth Bank

  https://www.bancorpsouth.com/

- Bank of Hawaii

  https://www.boh.com/

- East West Bank

  https://www.eastwestbank.com

- Fulton Bank

  https://www.fultonbank.com/

- Great Western Bank

  https://www.greatwesternbank.com

- Home Savings Bank

  https://www.homesavings.com/

- Independent Bank

  https://www.independentbank.com

- Midwest Bank

  https://www.midwestbank.net

- Old National Bank

  https://www.oldnational.com/

- Pacific Premier Bank

  https://www.ppbi.com

- Park National Bank

  https://www.parknationalbank.com/

- PlainsCapital Bank

  https://www.plainscapital.com

- Provident Bank

https://www.provident.bank/

- Renasant Bank

  https://www.provident.bank/

- South State Bank

  https://www.southstatebank.com

- Sterling Bank

  https://www.bankwithsterling.com/

- Texas Capital Bank

  https://www.texascapitalbank.com

- Trustmark National Bank

  http://www.trustmark.com/

- United Community Bank

  https://www.ucbi.com

- Webster Five

  https://www.web5.com

- WesBanco Bank

  https://www.wesbanco.com/

- Western Alliance Bank

  http://www.westernalliancebancorporation.com/

- Woodforest National Bank

  https://www.woodforest.com/

- Bank of Marin

  https://www.bankofmarin.com/

- Bridge Bank

  https://www.bridgebank.com/

- Cambridge Savings Bank

  https://www.cambridgesavings.com/

- Columbia Bank

  https://www.columbiabank.com

- EagleBank

  https://www.eaglebankcorp.com/

- First Bank

https://www.firstbanknj.com/

- First Merchants Bank

  https://www.firstmerchants.com/

- First National Bank of Pennsylvania

  https://www.fnb-online.com/

- First Security Bank

  https://www.fsbmsla.com

- First National Bank of Pennsylvania

  https://www.fnb-online.com/

- First Security Bank

  https://www.fsbmsla.com/

- Glacier Bank

  https://www.glacierbank.com

- Great Southern Bank

  https://www.greatsouthernbank.com/

- Heritage Bank

  https://www.heritagebanknw.com/

- HomeStreet Bank

  https://www.homestreet.com/

- Metro City Bank

  https://www.metrocitybank.bank.com/

- Middlesex Savings Bank

  https://www.middlesexbank.com

- New Resource Bank

  https://www.newresourcebank.com/

- North Shore Bank

  https://www.northshorebank.com

- OceanFirst Bank

  https://www.oceanfirst.com/

- Pacific Premier Bank

  https://www.ppbi.com/

- Peapack-Gladstone Bank

https://www.pgbank.com

- Provident Bank

    https://www.provident.bank/

- Rockland Trust

    https://www.rocklandtrust.com/

- Silicon Valley Bank

    https://www.svb.com/

- Skyline National Bank

    https://www.skylinenationalbank.com/

- South State Bank

    https://www.southstatebank.com/

- State Bank of Cross Plains

    https://www.crossplainsbank.com/

- Navy Federal Credit Union

    https://www.navyfederal.org/

- Alliant Credit Union

    https://www.alliantcreditunion.org

- Patelco Credit Union

    https://www.patelco.org/

- Security Service Federal Credit Union

    https://www.ssfcu.org/

- BECU

    https://www.becu.org/

- PenFed Credit Union

    https://www.penfed.org/

- Golden 1 Credit Union

    https://www.golden1.com/

- SchoolsFirst Federal Credit Union

    https://www.schoolsfirstfcu.org/

- First Tech Federal Credit Union

    https://www.firsttechfed.com/

- America First Credit Union
    https://www.americafirst.com/
- Travis Credit Union
    https://www.traviscu.org/
- Redwood Credit Union
    https://www.redwoodcu.org/
- SELCO Community Credit Union
    https://www.selco.org
- Visions Federal Credit Union
    https://www.visionsfcu.org/
- Desert Financial Credit Union
    https://www.desertfinancial.com/
- VyStar Credit Union
    https://vystarcu.org/
- Meridian Credit Union
    https://www.meridiancu.ca/
- Elevations Credit Union
    https://www.elevationscu.com/
- Kinecta Federal Credit Union
    https://www.kinecta.org/
- Firstmark Credit Union
    https://www.firstmarkcu.org/
- Wings Financial Credit Union
    https://www.wingsfinancial.com/
- Patelco Credit Union
    https://www.patelco.org/
- Lake Michigan Credit Union
    https://www.lmcu.org/
- GTE Financial
    https://www.gtefinancial.org/
- Oregon Community Credit Union
    https://www.oregoncommunitycu.org/

- South Carolina Federal Credit Union
  https://www.scfederal.org/
- Summit Credit Union
  https://www.summitcreditunion.com/
- Allegacy Federal Credit Union
  https://www.allegacy.org/
- Coastal Credit Union
  https://www.coastal24.com/
- Truliant Federal Credit Union
  https://www.truliantfcu.org
- FAIRWINDS Credit Union
  https://www.fairwinds.org
- Empower Federal Credit Union
  https://www.empowerfcu.com
- Tinker Federal Credit Union
  https://www.tinkerfcu.org/
- Aspire Federal Credit Union
  https://www.aspirefcu.org
- Idaho Central Credit Union
  https://www.iccu.com/
- America's First Federal Credit Union
  https://www.amfirst.org/
- America's Credit Union
  https://www.youracu.org/
- Delta Community Credit Union
  https://www.deltacommunitycu.com/
- San Diego County Credit Union
  https://www.sdccu.com/
- Redstone Federal Credit Union
  https://www.redfcu.org/
- Idaho Central Credit Union
  https://www.iccu.com/

- Numerica Credit Union

    https://www.numericacu.com/

- Arrowhead Credit Union

    https://www.arrowheadcu.org/

- First Commonwealth Federal Credit Union

    https://www.firstcomcu.org/

- Adiva Credit Union

    https://www.adivacu.org/

- Ascentra Credit Union

    https://www.ascentra.org/

- Georgia's Own Credit Union

    https://www.georgiasown.org/

- Northwest Federal Credit Union

    https://onenevada.org/banking/checking

- ## **Vehicle Financing Lenders**

These financing options have minimum requirements in order to qualify for them...please read before applying.

Navy Federal Business Vehicle Loans

- No fees
- PG required
- No prepayment penalties
- Loan to value: new, up to 100%; used, up to 90%
- A review of the CARFAX Vehicle History Report so you can buy with confidence

Ally Car Financing

- Reports to Dun and Bradstreet, Experian, and Equifax
- Lease or Loan Terms
- EIN needed
- D&B number needed
- Apply in dealership only (dealerships listed on the website)
- Need to establish business credit with D&B and Experian
- 2 tradelines over $10,000 reporting

Bank of America

- Loan amounts start at 10K
- PG required
- 48-72 terms
- Minimum vehicle value of $10,000
- Maximum vehicle age of 5 years
- Less than 75,000 miles

Ford Car Financing

- Reports to Dun and Bradstreet, Experian, and Equifax
- Lease or Loan Terms
- EIN needed
- D&B number needed

- At least 10 trade accounts reporting
- 1-2 trade accounts must be over $10K, if not PG may be required

Penske

- Reports to Dun and Bradstreet, Experian and Equifax
- Lease or Loan Terms
- EIN needed
- D& B number needed
- At least 10 trade accounts reporting
- 1-2 trade accounts must be over $10K, if not PG may be required

Ryder

- Reports to Dun and Bradstreet, Experian and Equifax
- Lease or Loan Terms
- EIN needed
- D& B number needed
- At least 10 trade accounts reporting
- 1-2 trade accounts must be over $10K, if not PG may be required

Toyota

Paper App: toyotafinancial.com/content/dam/tmcc-webcommons/toyotafinancial/documents/financing_options/for_business_credit_application/F7300.pdf

- Reports to Experian
- Lease or Loan Terms
- EIN needed
- D&B number needed
- At least 10 trade accounts reporting
- 1-2 trade accounts must be over $10K, if not PG may be required

Chrysler Capital Group

Commercial Number: 855-541-7744

- Reports to Dun and Bradstreet, Experian and Equifax
- Lease or Loan Terms
- EIN needed
- D& B number needed
- At least 10 trade accounts reporting
- 1-2 trade accounts must be over $10K. If not, PG may be required

Mercedes

- Reports to Experian
- Lease or Loan Terms
- EIN needed
- LLC or Corp 12 months old
- At least 10 trade accounts reporting
- 1-2 trade accounts must be over $10K. If not, PG may be required

• 26 U.S. CODE § 7702
LIFE INSURANCE CONTRACT DEFINED

•

•

(a) GENERAL RULE

For purposes of this title, the term "life insurance contract" means any contract which is a life insurance contract under the applicable law, but only if such contract —

(1) meets the cash value accumulation test of subsection (b), or

(2)

 (A) meets the guideline premium requirements of subsection (c), and

 (B) falls within the cash value corridor of subsection (d).

(b) CASH VALUE ACCUMULATION TEST FOR SUBSECTION (A)(1)

(1) IN GENERAL

A contract meets the cash value accumulation test of this subsection if, by the terms of the contract, the cash surrender value of such contract may not at any time exceed the net single premium which would have to be paid at such time to fund future beneQts under the contract.

(2) RULES FOR APPLYING PARAGRAPH (1)

Determinations under paragraph (1) shall be made—

(A) on the basis of interest at the greater of the applicable accumulation test minimum rate or the rate or rates guaranteed on issuance of the contract,

(B) on the basis of the rules of subparagraph (B)(i) (and, in the case of qualified additional benefits, subparagraph (B)(ii)) of subsection (c)(3), and

(C) by taking into account under subparagraphs (A) and (D) of subsection (e)(1) only current and future death benefits and qualified additional benefits.

(3) APPLICABLE ACCUMULATION TEST MINIMUM RATE

For purposes of paragraph (2)(A), the term "applicable accumulation test minimum rate" means the lesser of—

(A) an annual effective rate of 4 percent, or

(B) the insurance interest rate (as defined in subsection (f)(11)) in effect at the time the contract is issued.

(c) GUIDELINE PREMIUM REQUIREMENTS

For purposes of this section—

(1) IN GENERAL

A contract meets the guideline premium requirements of this subsection if the sum of the premiums paid under such contract does not at any time exceed the guideline premium limitation as of such time.

(2) GUIDELINE PREMIUM LIMITATION

The term "guideline premium limitation" means, as of any date, the greater of—

(A) the guideline single premium, or

(B) the sum of the guideline level premiums to such date.

(3) GUIDELINE SINGLE PREMIUM

(A) In general

The term "guideline single premium" means the premium at issue with respect to future benefits under the contract.

(B) Basis on which determination is made

The determination under subparagraph (A) shall be based on—

(i) reasonable mortality charges which meet the requirements prescribed in regulations to be promulgated by the Secretary or that do not exceed the mortality charges specified in the prevailing commissioners' standard tables as defined in subsection (f)(10),

(ii) any reasonable charges (other than mortality charges) which (on the basis of the company's experience, if any, with respect to similar contracts) are reasonably expected to be actually paid, and

(iii) interest at the greater of the applicable guideline premium minimum rate or the rate or rates guaranteed on issuance of the contract.

(C) When determination made

Except as provided in subsection (f)(7), the determination under subparagraph (A) shall be made as of the time the contract is issued.

(D) Special rules for subparagraph (B)(ii)

(i) Charges not specified in the contract

If any charge is not specified in the contract, the amount taken into account under subparagraph (B)(ii) for such charge shall be zero.

(ii) New companies, etc.

If any company does not have adequate experience for purposes of the determination under subparagraph (B)(ii), to the extent provided in regulations, such determination shall be made on the basis of the industry-wide experience.

(E) Applicable guideline premium minimum rate

For purposes of subparagraph (B)(iii), the term "applicable guideline premium minimum rate" means the applicable accumulation test minimum rate (as defined in subsection (b)(3)) plus 2 percentage points.

(4) GUIDELINE LEVEL PREMIUM

The term "guideline level premium" means the level annual amount, payable over a period not ending before the insured attains age 95, computed on the same basis as the guideline single premium, except that paragraph (3)(B)(iii) shall be applied by substituting "the applicable accumulation test minimum rate" for "the applicable guideline premium minimum rate".

(d) CASH VALUE CORRIDOR FOR PURPOSES OF SUBSECTION (A)(2)(B)

For purposes of this section—

(1) IN GENERAL

A contract falls within the cash value corridor of this subsection if the death benefit under the contract at any time is not less than the applicable percentage of the cash surrender value.

(2) APPLICABLE PERCENTAGE

In the case of an insured with an attained age as of the beginning of the contract year of:		The applicable percentage shall decrease by a ratable portion for each full year:	
More than:	But not more than:	From:	To:
0	40	250	250
40	45	250	215
45	50	215	185
50	55	185	150
55	60	150	130
60	65	130	120
65	70	120	115
70	75	115	105
75	90	105	105
90	95	105	100.

(e) COMPUTATIONAL RULES

(1) IN GENERAL

For purposes of this section (other than subsection (d))—

(A) the death benefit (and any qualified additional benefit) shall be deemed not to increase,

(B) the maturity date, including the date on which any benefit described in subparagraph (C) is payable, shall be deemed to be no earlier than the day on which the insured attains age 95, and no later than the day on which the insured attains age 100,

(C) the death benefits shall be deemed to be provided until the maturity date determined by taking into account subparagraph (B), and

(D) the amount of any endowment benefit (or sum of endowment benefits, including any cash surrender value on the maturity date determined by taking into account subparagraph (B)) shall be deemed not to exceed the least amount payable as a death benefit at any time under the contract.

(2) LIMITED INCREASES IN DEATH BENEFIT PERMITTED

Notwithstanding paragraph (1)(A)—

(A) for purposes of computing the guideline level premium, an increase in the death benefit which is provided in the contract may be taken into account but only to the extent necessary to prevent a decrease in the excess of the death benefit over the cash surrender value of the contract,

(B) for purposes of the cash value accumulation test, the increase described in subparagraph (A) may be taken into account if the contract will meet such test at all times assuming that the net level reserve (determined as if level annual premiums were paid for the contract over a period not ending before the insured attains age 95) is substituted for the net single premium, and

(C) for purposes of the cash value accumulation test, the death benefit increases may be taken into account if the contract—

  (i) has an initial death benefit of $5,000 or less and a maximum death benefit of $25,000 or less,

  (ii) provides for a fixed predetermined annual increase not to exceed 10 percent of the initial death benefit or 8 percent of the death benefit at the end of the preceding year, and

  (iii) was purchased to cover payment of burial expenses or in connection with prearranged funeral expenses.

For purposes of subparagraph (C), the initial death benefit of a contract shall be determined by treating all contracts issued to the same contract owner as 1 contract.

(f) OTHER DEFINITIONS AND SPECIAL RULES

For purposes of this section—

(1) PREMIUMS PAID

  (A) In general

The term "premiums paid" means the premiums paid under the contract less amounts (other than amounts includible in gross income) to which section 72(e) applies and less any excess premiums with respect to which there is a distribution described in subparagraph (B) or (E) of paragraph (7) and any other amounts received with respect to the contract which are specified in regulations.

(B) Treatment of certain premiums returned to policyholder

If, in order to comply with the requirements of subsection (a)(2)(A), any portion of any premium paid during any contract year is returned by the insurance company (with interest) within 60 days after the end of a contract year, the amount so returned (excluding interest) shall be deemed to reduce the sum of the premiums paid under the contract during such year.

(C) Interest returned includible in gross income

Notwithstanding the provisions of section 72(e), the amount of any interest returned as provided in subparagraph (B) shall be includible in the gross income of the recipient.

(2) CASH VALUES

(A) Cash surrender value

The cash surrender value of any contract shall be its cash value determined without regard to any surrender charge, policy loan, or reasonable termination dividends.

(B) Net surrender value

The net surrender value of any contract shall be determined with regard to surrender charges but without regard to any policy loan.

(3) DEATH BENEFIT

The term "death benefit" means the amount payable by reason of the death of the insured (determined without regard to any qualified additional benefits).

(4) FUTURE BENEFITS

The term "future benefits" means death benefits and endowment benefits.

(5) QUALIFIED ADDITIONAL BENEFITS

(A) In general

The term "qualified additional benefits" means any—

(i) guaranteed insurability,

(ii) accidental death or disability benefit,

(iii) family term coverage,

(iv) disability waiver benefit, or

(v) other benefit prescribed under regulations.

(B) Treatment of qualified additional benefits

For purposes of this section, qualified additional benefits shall not be treated as future benefits under the contract, but the charges for such benefits shall be treated as future benefits.

(C) Treatment of other additional benefits

In the case of any additional benefit which is not a qualified additional benefit—

(i) such benefit shall not be treated as a future benefit, and

(ii) any charge for such benefit which is not prefunded shall not be treated as a premium.

(6) Premium payments not disqualifying contract

The payment of a premium which would result in the sum of the premiums paid exceeding the guideline premium limitation shall be disregarded for purposes of subsection (a)(2) if the amount of such premium does not exceed the amount necessary to prevent the termination of the contract on or before the end of the contract year (but only if the contract will have no cash surrender value at the end of such extension period).

(7) Adjustments

(A) In general

If there is a change in the benefits under (or in other terms of) the contract which was not reflected in any previous determination or adjustment made under this section, there shall be proper adjustments in future determinations made under this section.

(B) Rule for certain changes during first 15 years

If—

(i) a change described in subparagraph (A) reduces benefits under the contract,

Under regulations prescribed by the Secretary, subparagraph (B) shall apply also to any distribution made in anticipation of a reduction in benefits under the contract. For purposes of the preceding sentence, appropriate adjustments shall be made in the provisions of subparagraphs (C) and (D); and any distribution which reduces the cash surrender value of a contract and which is made within 2 years before a reduction in benefits under the contract shall be treated as made in anticipation of such reduction.

(8) CORRECTION OF ERRORS

If the taxpayer establishes to the satisfaction of the Secretary that—

(A) the requirements described in subsection (a) for any contract year were not satisfied due to reasonable error, and

(B) reasonable steps are being taken to remedy the error,

the Secretary may waive the failure to satisfy such requirements.

(9) SPECIAL RULE FOR VARIABLE LIFE INSURANCE CONTRACTS

In the case of any contract which is a variable contract (as defined in section 817), the determination of whether such contract meets the requirements of subsection (a) shall be made whenever the death benefits under such contract change but not less frequently than once during each 12-month period.

(10) PREVAILING COMMISSIONERS' STANDARD TABLES

For purposes of subsection (c)(3)(B)(i), the term "prevailing commissioners' standard tables" means the most recent commissioners' standard tables prescribed by the National Association of Insurance Commissioners which are permitted to be used in computing reserves for that type of contract under the insurance laws of at least 26 States when the contract was issued. If the prevailing commissioners' standard tables as of the beginning of any calendar year (hereinafter in this paragraph referred to as the "year of change") are different from the prevailing commissioners' standard tables as of the beginning of the preceding calendar year, the issuer may use the prevailing commissioners' standard tables as of the beginning of the preceding calendar year with respect to any contract issued after the change and before the close of the 3-year period beginning on the first day of the year of change.

(11) INSURANCE INTEREST RATE

For purposes of this section—

(A) In general

The term "insurance interest rate" means, with respect to any contract issued

(ii) the change occurs during the 15-year period beginning on the issue date of the contract, and

(iii) a cash distribution is made to the policyholder as a result of such change,

section 72 (other than subsection (e)(5) thereof) shall apply to such cash distribution to the extent it does not exceed the recapture ceiling determined under subparagraph (C) or (D) (whichever applies).

(C) Recapture ceiling where change occurs during first 5 years

If the change referred to in subparagraph (B)(ii) occurs during the 5-year period beginning on the issue date of the contract, the recapture ceiling is—

(i) in the case of a contract to which subsection (a)(1) applies, the excess of—

(I) the cash surrender value of the contract, immediately before the reduction, over

(II) the net single premium (determined under subsection (b)), immediately after the reduction, or

(ii) in the case of a contract to which subsection (a)(2) applies, the greater of—

(I) the excess of the aggregate premiums paid under the contract, immediately before the reduction, over the guideline premium limitation for the contract (determined under subsection (c)(2), taking into account the adjustment described in subparagraph (A)), or

(II) the excess of the cash surrender value of the contract, immediately before the reduction, over the cash value corridor of subsection (d) (determined immediately after the reduction).

(D) Recapture ceiling where change occurs after 5th year and before 16th year

If the change referred to in subparagraph (B) occurs after the 5-year period referred to under subparagraph (C), the recapture ceiling is the excess of the cash surrender value of the contract, immediately before the reduction, over the cash value corridor of subsection (d) (determined immediately after the reduction and whether or not subsection (d) applies to the contract).

(E) Treatment of certain distributions made in anticipation of benefit reductions

in any calendar year, the lesser of—

(i) the section 7702 valuation interest rate for such calendar year (or, if such calendar year is not an adjustment year, the most recent adjustment year), or

(ii) the section 7702 applicable Federal interest rate for such calendar year (or, if such calendar year is not an adjustment year, the most recent adjustment year).

(B) Section 7702 valuation interest rate

The term "section 7702 valuation interest rate" means, with respect to any adjustment year, the prescribed U.S. valuation interest rate for life insurance with guaranteed durations of more than 20 years (as defined in the National Association of Insurance Commissioners' Standard Valuation Law) as effective in the calendar year immediately preceding such adjustment year.

(C) Section 7702 applicable Federal interest rate

The term "section 7702 applicable Federal interest rate" means, with respect to any adjustment year, the average (rounded to the nearest whole percentage point) of the applicable Federal mid-term rates (as defined in section 1274(d) but based on annual compounding) effective as of the beginning of each of the calendar months in the most recent 60-month period ending before the second calendar year prior to such adjustment year.

(D) Adjustment year

The term "adjustment year" means the calendar year following any calendar year that includes the effective date of a change in the prescribed U.S. valuation interest rate for life insurance with guaranteed durations of more than 20 years (as defined in the National Association of Insurance Commissioners' Standard Valuation Law).

(E) Transition rule

Notwithstanding subparagraph (A), the insurance interest rate shall be 2 percent in the case of any contract which is issued during the period that—

(i) begins on January 1, 2021, and

(ii) ends immediately before the beginning of the first adjustment year that beings [1] after December 31, 2021.

(g) Treatment of contracts which do not meet subsection (a) test

(1) Income inclusion

(A) In general

If at any time any contract which is a life insurance contract under the applicable law does not meet the definition of life insurance contract under subsection (a), the income on the contract for any taxable year of the policyholder shall be treated as ordinary income received or accrued by the policyholder during such year.

(B) Income on the contract

For purposes of this paragraph, the term "income on the contract" means, with respect to any taxable year of the policyholder, the excess of—

(i) the sum of—

(I) the increase in the net surrender value of the contract during the taxable year, and

(II) the cost of life insurance protection provided under the contract during the taxable year, over

(ii) the premiums paid (as defined in subsection (f)(1)) under the contract during the taxable year.

(C) Contracts which cease to meet definition

If, during any taxable year of the policyholder, a contract which is a life insurance contract under the applicable law ceases to meet the definition of life insurance contract under subsection (a), the income on the contract for all prior taxable years shall be treated as received or accrued during the taxable year in which such cessation occurs.

(D) Cost of life insurance protection

For purposes of this paragraph, the cost of life insurance protection provided under the contract shall be the lesser of—

(i) the cost of individual insurance on the life of the insured as determined on the basis of uniform premiums (computed on the basis of 5-year age brackets) prescribed by the Secretary by regulations, or

(ii) the mortality charge (if any) stated in the contract.

(2) TREATMENT OF AMOUNT PAID ON DEATH OF INSURED

If any contract which is a life insurance contract under the applicable law does not meet the definition of life insurance contract under subsection (a), the excess of the amount paid by the reason of the death of the insured over the net surrender value of the contract shall be deemed to be paid under a life insurance contract for purposes of section 101 and subtitle B.

(3) CONTRACT CONTINUES TO BE TREATED AS INSURANCE CONTRACT
If any contract which is a life insurance contract under the applicable law does not meet the definition of life insurance contract under subsection (a), such contract shall, notwithstanding such failure, be treated as an insurance contract for purposes of this title.

(h) ENDOWMENT CONTRACTS RECEIVE SAME TREATMENT

(1) IN GENERAL
References in subsections (a) and (g) to a life insurance contract shall be treated as including references to a contract which is an endowment contract under the applicable law.

(2) DEFINITION OF ENDOWMENT CONTRACT
For purposes of this title (other than paragraph (1)), the term "endowment contract" means a contract which is an endowment contract under the applicable law and which meets the requirements of subsection (a).

(i) TRANSITIONAL RULE FOR CERTAIN 20-PAY CONTRACTS

(1) IN GENERAL
In the case of a qualified 20-pay contract, this section shall be applied by substituting "3 percent" for "4 percent" in subsection (b)(2).

(2) QUALIFIED 20-PAY CONTRACT
For purposes of paragraph (1), the term "qualified 20-pay contract" means any contract which—

(A) requires at least 20 nondecreasing annual premium payments, and

(B) is issued pursuant to an existing plan of insurance.

(3) EXISTING PLAN OF INSURANCE
For purposes of this subsection, the term "existing plan of insurance" means, with respect to any contract, any plan of insurance which was filed by the company issuing such contract in 1 or more States before September 28, 1983, and is on file in the appropriate State for such contract.

(j) CERTAIN CHURCH SELF-FUNDED DEATH BENEFIT PLANS TREATED AS LIFE INSURANCE

(1) IN GENERAL

In determining whether any plan or arrangement described in paragraph (2) is a life insurance contract, the requirement of subsection (a) that the contract be a life insurance contract under applicable law shall not apply.

(2) DESCRIPTION

For purposes of this subsection, a plan or arrangement is described in this paragraph if—

(A) such plan or arrangement provides for the payment of benefits by reason of the death of the individuals covered under such plan or arrangement, and

(B) such plan or arrangement is provided by a church for the benefit of its employees and their beneficiaries, directly or through an organization described in section 414(e)(3)(A) or an organization described in section 414(e)(3)(B)(ii).

(3) DEFINITIONS

For purposes of this subsection—

(A) Church

The term "church" means a church or a convention or association of churches.

(B) Employee

The term "employee" includes an employee described in section 414(e)(3)(B).

(k) REGULATIONS

The Secretary shall prescribe such regulations as may be necessary or appropriate to carry out the purposes of this section.

(Added Pub. L. 98–369, div. A, title II, § 221(a), July 18, 1984, 98 Stat. 767; amended Pub. L. 99–514, title XVIII, § 1825(a)–(c), Oct. 22, 1986, 100 Stat. 2846–2848; Pub. L. 100–647, title V, § 5011(a), (b), title VI, § 6078(a), Nov. 10, 1988, 102 Stat. 3660, 3661, 3709; Pub. L. 115–97, title I, § 13517(a)(4), Dec. 22, 2017, 131 Stat. 2146; Pub. L. 116–260, div. EE, title II, § 205(a)–(d), Dec. 27, 2020, 134 Stat. 3058.)

• 15 U.S. CODE § 1681B
PERMISSIBLE PURPOSES OF CONSUMER REPORTS

(a) IN GENERAL

Subject to subsection (c), any consumer reporting agency may furnish a consumer report under the following circumstances and no other:

(1) In response to the order of a court having jurisdiction to issue such an order, a subpoena issued in connection with proceedings before a Federal grand jury, or a subpoena issued in accordance with section 5318 of title 31 or section 3486 of title 18.

(2) In accordance with the written instructions of the consumer to whom it relates.

(3) To a person which it has reason to believe—

(A) intends to use the information in connection with a credit transaction involving the consumer on whom the information is to be furnished and involving the extension of credit to, or review or collection of an account of, the consumer; or

(B) intends to use the information for employment purposes; or

(C) intends to use the information in connection with the underwriting of insurance involving the consumer; or

(D) intends to use the information in connection with a determination of the consumer's eligibility for a license or other benefit granted by a governmental instrumentality required by law to consider an applicant's financial responsibility or status; or

•

(E) intends to use the information, as a potential investor or servicer, or current insurer, in connection with a valuation of, or an assessment of the <u>credit</u> or prepayment risks associated with, an existing <u>credit</u> obligation; or

(F) otherwise has a legitimate business need for the information—

(i) in connection with a business transaction that is initiated by the <u>consumer;</u> or

(ii) to review an <u>account</u> to determine whether the <u>consumer</u> continues to meet the terms of the <u>account.</u>

(G) executive departments and agencies in connection with the issuance of government-sponsored individually-billed travel charge cards.

(4) In response to a request by the head of a <u>State or local child support enforcement agency</u> (or a <u>State</u> or local government official authorized by the head of such an agency), if the <u>person</u> making the request certifies to the <u>consumer reporting agency</u> that—

(A) the <u>consumer report</u> is needed for the purpose of establishing an individual's capacity to make child support payments, determining the appropriate level of such payments, or enforcing a child support order, award, agreement, or judgment;

(B) the parentage of the <u>consumer</u> for the child to which the obligation relates has been established or acknowledged by the <u>consumer</u> in accordance with <u>State</u> laws under which the obligation arises (if required by those laws); and

(C) the <u>consumer report</u> will be kept confidential, will be used solely for a purpose described in subparagraph (A), and will not be used in connection with any other civil, administrative, or criminal proceeding, or for any other purpose.

(5) To an agency administering a <u>State</u> plan under <u>section 654 of title 42</u> for use to set an initial or modified child support award.

(6) To the Federal Deposit Insurance Corporation or the National Credit Union Administration as part of its preparation for its appointment or as part of its exercise of powers, as conservator, receiver, or liquidating agent for an insured depository institution or insured <u>credit</u> union under the <u>Federal Deposit Insurance Act</u> [12 U.S.C. <u>1811</u> et seq.] or the <u>Federal Credit Union Act</u> [12 U.S.C. 1751 et seq.], or other applicable Federal or <u>State</u> law, or in connection with the resolution or liquidation of a failed or failing insured depository institution or insured <u>credit</u> union, as applicable.

(b) Conditions for furnishing and using consumer reports for employment purposes

(1) Certification from user

A consumer reporting agency may furnish a consumer report for employment purposes only if—

(A) the person who obtains such report from the agency certifies to the agency that—

(i) the person has complied with paragraph (2) with respect to the consumer report, and the person will comply with paragraph (3) with respect to the consumer report if paragraph (3) becomes applicable; and

(ii) information from the consumer report will not be used in violation of any applicable Federal or State equal employment opportunity law or regulation; and

(B) the consumer reporting agency provides with the report, or has previously provided, a summary of the consumer's rights under this subchapter, as prescribed by the Bureau under section 1681g(c)(3) [1] of this title.

(2) Disclosure to consumer

(A) In general

Except as provided in subparagraph (B), a person may not procure a consumer report, or cause a consumer report to be procured, for employment purposes with respect to any consumer, unless—

(i) a clear and conspicuous disclosure has been made in writing to the consumer at any time before the report is procured or caused to be procured, in a document that consists solely of the disclosure, that a consumer report may be obtained for employment purposes; and

(ii) the consumer has authorized in writing (which authorization may be made on the document referred to in clause (i)) the procurement of the report by that person.

(B) Application by mail, telephone, computer, or other similar means

If a consumer described in subparagraph (C) applies for employment by mail, telephone, computer, or other similar means, at any time before a consumer report is procured or caused to be procured in connection with that application—

(i) the person who procures the consumer report on the consumer for employment purposes shall provide to the consumer, by oral, written, or electronic means, notice that a consumer report may be obtained for employment purposes, and a summary of the consumer's rights under section 1681m(a)(3) [1] of this title; and

(ii) the consumer shall have consented, orally, in writing, or electronically to the procurement of the report by that person.

(C) Scope

Subparagraph (B) shall apply to a person procuring a consumer report on a consumer in connection with the consumer's application for employment only if—

(i) the consumer is applying for a position over which the Secretary of Transportation has the power to establish qualifications and maximum hours of service pursuant to the provisions of section 31502 of title 49, or a position subject to safety regulation by a State transportation agency; and

(ii) as of the time at which the person procures the report or causes the report to be procured the only interaction between the consumer and the person in connection with that employment application has been by mail, telephone, computer, or other similar means.

(3) CONDITIONS ON USE FOR ADVERSE ACTIONS

(A) In general

Except as provided in subparagraph (B), in using a consumer report for employment purposes, before taking any adverse action based in whole or in part on the report, the person intending to take such adverse action shall provide to the consumer to whom the report relates—

(i) a copy of the report; and

(ii) a description in writing of the rights of the consumer under this subchapter, as prescribed by the Bureau under section 1681g(c)(3) [1] of this title.

(B) Application by mail, telephone, computer, or other similar means

(i) If a consumer described in subparagraph (C) applies for employment by mail, telephone, computer, or other similar means, and if a person who has procured a consumer report on the consumer for employment purposes takes adverse action on the employment application based in whole or in part on the report, then the person must provide to the consumer to whom the report relates, in lieu of the notices required under subparagraph (A) of this section and under section 1681m(a) of this title, within 3 business days of taking such action, an oral, written or electronic notification—

(I) that adverse action has been taken based in whole or in part on a consumer report received from a consumer reporting agency;

(II) of the name, address and telephone number of the consumer reporting agency that furnished the consumer report (including a toll-free telephone number established by the agency if the agency compiles and maintains files on consumers on a nationwide basis);

(III) that the consumer reporting agency did not make the decision to take the adverse action and is unable to provide to the consumer the specific reasons why the adverse action was taken; and

(IV) that the consumer may, upon providing proper identification, request a free copy of a report and may dispute with the consumer reporting agency the accuracy or completeness of any information in a report.

(ii) If, under clause (B)(i)(IV), the consumer requests a copy of a consumer report from the person who procured the report, then, within 3 business days of receiving the consumer's request, together with proper identification, the person must send or provide to the consumer a copy of a report and a copy of the consumer's rights as prescribed by the Bureau under section 1681g(c)(3)[1] of this title.

(C) Scope

Subparagraph (B) shall apply to a person procuring a consumer report on a consumer in connection with the consumer's application for employment only if—

(i) the consumer is applying for a position over which the Secretary of Transportation has the power to establish qualifications and maximum hours of service pursuant to the provisions of section 31502 of title 49, or a position subject to safety regulation by a State transportation agency; and

(ii) as of the time at which the person procures the report or causes the report to be procured the only interaction between the consumer and the person in connection with that employment application has been by mail, telephone, computer, or other similar means.

(4) EXCEPTION FOR NATIONAL SECURITY INVESTIGATIONS

(A) In general

In the case of an agency or department of the United States Government which seeks to obtain and use a consumer report for employment purposes, paragraph (3) shall not apply to any adverse action by such agency or department which is based in part on such consumer report, if the head of such agency or department makes a written finding that—

(i) the consumer report is relevant to a national security investigation of such agency or department;

(ii) the investigation is within the jurisdiction of such agency or department;

(iii) there is reason to believe that compliance with paragraph (3) will—

(I) endanger the life or physical safety of any person;

(II) result in flight from prosecution;

(III) result in the destruction of, or tampering with, evidence relevant to the investigation;

(IV) result in the intimidation of a potential witness relevant to the investigation;

(V) result in the compromise of classified information; or

(VI) otherwise seriously jeopardize or unduly delay the investigation or another official proceeding.

(B) Notification of consumer upon conclusion of investigation

Upon the conclusion of a national security investigation described in subparagraph (A), or upon the determination that the exception under subparagraph (A) is no longer required for the reasons set forth in such subparagraph, the official exercising the authority in such subparagraph shall provide to the consumer who is the subject of the consumer report with regard to which such finding was made—

(i) a copy of such consumer report with any classified information redacted as necessary;

(ii) notice of any adverse action which is based, in part, on the consumer report; and

(iii) the identification with reasonable specificity of the nature of the investigation for which the consumer report was sought.

(C) Delegation by head of agency or department

For purposes of subparagraphs (A) and (B), the head of any agency or department of the United States Government may delegate his or her authorities under this paragraph to an official of such agency or department who has personnel security responsibilities and is a member of the Senior Executive Service or equivalent civilian or military rank.

(D) Definitions

For purposes of this paragraph, the following definitions shall apply:

(i) Classified information

The term "classified information" means information that is protected from unauthorized disclosure under Executive Order No. 12958 or successor orders.

(ii) National security investigation

The term "national security investigation" means any official inquiry by an agency or department of the United States Government to determine the eligibility of a consumer to receive access or continued access to classified information or to determine whether classified information has been lost or compromised.

(c) FURNISHING REPORTS IN CONNECTION WITH CREDIT OR INSURANCE TRANSACTIONS THAT ARE NOT INITIATED BY CONSUMER

(1) IN GENERAL

A consumer reporting agency may furnish a consumer report relating to any consumer pursuant to subparagraph (A) or (C) of subsection (a)(3) in connection with any credit or insurance transaction that is not initiated by the consumer only if—

(A) the consumer authorizes the agency to provide such report to such person; or

(B)

(i) the transaction consists of a firm offer of credit or insurance;

(ii) the consumer reporting agency has complied with subsection (e);

(iii) there is not in effect an election by the consumer, made in accordance with subsection (e), to have the consumer's name and address excluded from lists of names provided by the agency pursuant to this paragraph; and

(iv) the consumer report does not contain a date of birth that shows that the consumer has not attained the age of 21, or, if the date of birth on the consumer report shows that the consumer has not attained the age of 21, such consumer consents to the consumer reporting agency to such furnishing.

(2) LIMITS ON INFORMATION RECEIVED UNDER PARAGRAPH (1)(B)

A person may receive pursuant to paragraph (1)(B) only—

(A) the name and address of a consumer;

(B) an identifier that is not unique to the consumer and that is used by the person solely for the purpose of verifying the identity of the consumer; and

(C) other information pertaining to a consumer that does not identify the relationship or experience of the consumer with respect to a particular creditor or other entity.

(3) INFORMATION REGARDING INQUIRIES

Except as provided in section 1681g(a)(5) of this title, a consumer reporting agency shall not furnish to any person a record of inquiries in connection with a credit or insurance transaction that is not initiated by a consumer.

(d) RESERVED

(e) ELECTION OF CONSUMER TO BE EXCLUDED FROM LISTS

(1) IN GENERAL

A consumer may elect to have the consumer's name and address excluded from any list provided by a consumer reporting agency under subsection (c)(1)(B) in connection with a credit or insurance transaction that is not initiated by the consumer, by notifying the agency in accordance with paragraph (2) that the consumer does not consent to any use of a consumer report relating to the consumer in connection with any credit or insurance transaction that is not initiated by the consumer.

(2) MANNER OF NOTIFICATION

A consumer shall notify a consumer reporting agency under paragraph (1)—

(A) through the notification system maintained by the agency under paragraph (5); or

(B) by submitting to the agency a signed notice of election form issued by the agency for purposes of this subparagraph.

(3) RESPONSE OF AGENCY AFTER NOTIFICATION THROUGH SYSTEM

Upon receipt of notification of the election of a consumer under paragraph (1) through the notification system maintained by the agency under paragraph (5), a consumer reporting agency shall—

(A) inform the consumer that the election is effective only for the 5-year period following the election if the consumer does not submit to the agency a signed notice of election form issued by the agency for purposes of paragraph (2)(B); and

(B) provide to the consumer a notice of election form, if requested by the consumer, not later than 5 business days after receipt of the notification of the election through the system established under paragraph (5), in the case of a request made at the time the consumer provides notification through the system.

(4) EFFECTIVENESS OF ELECTION

An election of a consumer under paragraph (1)—

(A) shall be effective with respect to a consumer reporting agency beginning 5 business days after the date on which the consumer notifies the agency in accordance with paragraph (2);

(B) shall be effective with respect to a consumer reporting agency—

(i) subject to subparagraph (C), during the 5-year period beginning 5 business days after the date on which the consumer notifies the agency of the election, in the case of an election for which a consumer notifies the agency only in accordance with paragraph (2)(A); or

(ii) until the consumer notifies the agency under subparagraph (C), in the case of an election for which a consumer notifies the agency in accordance with paragraph (2)(B);

(C) shall not be effective after the date on which the consumer notifies the agency, through the notification system established by the agency under paragraph (5), that the election is no longer effective; and

(D) shall be effective with respect to each affiliate of the agency.

(5) NOTIFICATION SYSTEM

(A) In general

Each consumer reporting agency that, under subsection (c)(1)(B), furnishes a consumer report in connection with a credit or insurance transaction that is not initiated by a consumer, shall—

(i) establish and maintain a notification system, including a toll-free telephone number, which permits any consumer whose consumer report is maintained by the agency to notify the agency, with appropriate identification, of the consumer's election to have the consumer's name and address excluded from any such list of names and addresses provided by the agency for such a transaction; and

(ii) publish by not later than 365 days after September 30, 1996, and not less than annually thereafter, in a publication of general circulation in the area served by the agency—

(I) a notification that information in consumer files maintained by the agency may be used in connection with such transactions; and

(II) the address and toll-free telephone number for consumers to use to notify the agency of the consumer's election under clause (i).

(B) Establishment and maintenance as compliance
Establishment and maintenance of a notification system (including a toll-free telephone number) and publication by a consumer reporting agency on the agency's own behalf and on behalf of any of its affiliates in accordance with this paragraph is deemed to be compliance with this paragraph by each of those affiliates.

(6) NOTIFICATION SYSTEM BY AGENCIES THAT OPERATE NATIONWIDE
Each consumer reporting agency that compiles and maintains files on consumers on a nationwide basis shall establish and maintain a notification system for purposes of paragraph (5) jointly with other such consumer reporting agencies.

(f) CERTAIN USE OR OBTAINING OF INFORMATION PROHIBITED
A person shall not use or obtain a consumer report for any purpose unless—

(1) the consumer report is obtained for a purpose for which the consumer report is authorized to be furnished under this section; and

(2) the purpose is certified in accordance with section 1681e of this title by a prospective user of the report through a general or specific certification.

(g) PROTECTION OF MEDICAL INFORMATION

(1) LIMITATION ON CONSUMER REPORTING AGENCIES
A consumer reporting agency shall not furnish for employment purposes, or in

connection with a credit or insurance transaction, a consumer report that contains medical information (other than medical contact information treated in the manner required under section 1681c(a)(6) of this title) about a consumer, unless—

(A) if furnished in connection with an insurance transaction, the consumer affirmatively consents to the furnishing of the report;

(B) if furnished for employment purposes or in connection with a credit transaction—

    (i) the information to be furnished is relevant to process or effect the employment or credit transaction; and

    (ii) the consumer provides specific written consent for the furnishing of the report that describes in clear and conspicuous language the use for which the information will be furnished; or

(C) the information to be furnished pertains solely to transactions, accounts, or balances relating to debts arising from the receipt of medical services, products, or devises, where such information, other than account status or amounts, is restricted or reported using codes that do not identify, or do not provide information sufficient to infer, the specific provider or the nature of such services, products, or devices, as provided in section 1681c(a)(6) of this title.

(2) LIMITATION ON CREDITORS
Except as permitted pursuant to paragraph (3)(C) or regulations prescribed under paragraph (5)(A), a creditor shall not obtain or use medical information (other than medical information treated in the manner required under section 1681c(a)(6) of this title) pertaining to a consumer in connection with any determination of the consumer's eligibility, or continued eligibility, for credit.

(3) ACTIONS AUTHORIZED BY FEDERAL LAW, INSURANCE ACTIVITIES AND REGULATORY DETERMINATIONS
Section 1681a(d)(3) of this title shall not be construed so as to treat information or any communication of information as a consumer report if the information or communication is disclosed—

(A) in connection with the business of insurance or annuities, including the activities described in section 18B of the model Privacy of Consumer Financial and Health Information Regulation issued by the National Association of Insurance Commissioners (as in effect on January 1, 2003);

(B) for any purpose permitted without authorization under the Standards for Individually Identifiable Health Information promulgated by the Department of

Health and Human Services pursuant to the Health Insurance Portability and Accountability Act of 1996, or referred to under section 1179 of such Act,[1] or described in section 6802(e) of this title; or

(C) as otherwise determined to be necessary and appropriate, by regulation or order, by the Bureau or the applicable State insurance authority (with respect to any person engaged in providing insurance or annuities).

(4) LIMITATION ON REDISCLOSURE OF MEDICAL INFORMATION

Any person that receives medical information pursuant to paragraph (1) or (3) shall not disclose such information to any other person, except as necessary to carry out the purpose for which the information was initially disclosed, or as otherwise permitted by statute, regulation, or order.

(5) REGULATIONS AND EFFECTIVE DATE FOR PARAGRAPH **(2)**

(A) [2] **Regulations required**

The Bureau may, after notice and opportunity for comment, prescribe regulations that permit transactions under paragraph (2) that are determined to be necessary and appropriate to protect legitimate operational, transactional, risk, consumer, and other needs (and which shall include permitting actions necessary for administrative verification purposes), consistent with the intent of paragraph (2) to restrict the use of medical information for inappropriate purposes.

(6) COORDINATION WITH OTHER LAWS

No provision of this subsection shall be construed as altering, affecting, or superseding the applicability of any other provision of Federal law relating to medical confidentiality.

(Pub. L. 90–321, title VI, § 604, as added Pub. L. 91–508, title VI, § 601, Oct. 26, 1970, 84 Stat. 1129; amended Pub. L. 101–73, title IX, § 964(c), Aug. 9, 1989, 103 Stat. 506; Pub. L. 104–193, title III, § 352, Aug. 22, 1996, 110 Stat. 2240; Pub. L. 104–208, div. A, title II, §§ 2403, 2404(a), (b), 2405, Sept. 30, 1996, 110 Stat. 3009–430, 3009–431, 3009–433, 3009–434; Pub. L. 105–107, title III, § 311(a), Nov. 20, 1997, 111 Stat. 2255; Pub. L. 105–347, §§ 2, 3, 6(4), Nov. 2, 1998, 112 Stat. 3208, 3210, 3211; Pub. L. 107–306, title VIII, § 811(b)(8)(A), Nov. 27, 2002, 116 Stat. 2426; Pub. L. 108–159, title II, § 213(c), title IV, §§ 411(a), 412(f), title VIII, § 811(b), Dec. 4, 2003, 117 Stat. 1979, 1999, 2003, 2011; Pub. L. 108–177, title III, § 361(j), Dec. 13, 2003, 117 Stat. 2625; Pub. L. 109–351, title VII, § 719, Oct. 13, 2006, 120 Stat. 1998; Pub. L. 110–161, div. D, title VII, § 743, Dec. 26, 2007, 121 Stat. 2033; Pub. L. 111–24, title III, § 302, May 22, 2009, 123 Stat. 1748; Pub. L. 111–203, title X, § 1088(a)(2)(A), (4), July 21, 2010, 124 Stat. 2087; Pub. L. 114–94, div. G, title LXXX, § 80001, Dec. 4, 2015, 129 Stat. 1792; Pub. L. 116–283, div. F, title LXIII, § 6308(b), Jan. 1, 2021, 134 Stat. 4594.)

• 15 U.S. CODE § 1681C
REQUIREMENTS RELATING TO INFORMATION CONTAINED IN CONSUMER REPORTS

(a) INFORMATION EXCLUDED FROM CONSUMER REPORTS

Except as authorized under subsection (b), no consumer reporting agency may make any consumer report containing any of the following items of information:

(1) Cases under title 11 or under the Bankruptcy Act that, from the date of entry of the order for relief or the date of adjudication, as the case may be, antedate the report by more than 10 years.

(2) Civil suits, civil judgments, and records of arrest that, from date of entry, antedate the report by more than seven years or until the governing statute of limitations has expired, whichever is the longer period.

(3) Paid tax liens which, from date of payment, antedate the report by more than seven years.

(4) Accounts placed for collection or charged to profit and loss which antedate the report by more than seven years.

(5) Any other adverse item of information, other than records of convictions of crimes which antedates the report by more than seven years.

(6) The name, address, and telephone number of any medical information furnisher that has notified the agency of its status, unless—

(A) such name, address, and telephone number are restricted or reported using codes that do not identify, or provide information sufficient to infer, the specific provider or the nature of such services, products, or devices to a <u>person</u> other than the <u>consumer</u>; or

(B) the report is being provided to an insurance company for a purpose relating to engaging in the business of insurance other than property and casualty insurance.

(7) With respect to a <u>consumer reporting agency</u> described in <u>section 1681a(p) of this title</u>, any information related to a <u>veteran's</u> medical debt if the date on which the hospital care, medical services, or extended care services was rendered relating to the debt antedates the report by less than 1 year if the <u>consumer reporting agency</u> has actual knowledge that the information is related to a <u>veteran's</u> medical debt and the <u>consumer reporting agency</u> is in compliance with its obligation under section 302(c)(5) of the Economic Growth, Regulatory Relief, and Consumer Protection Act.

(8) With respect to a <u>consumer reporting agency</u> described in <u>section 1681a(p) of this title</u>, any information related to a fully paid or settled <u>veteran's</u> medical debt that had been characterized as delinquent, charged off, or in collection if the <u>consumer reporting agency</u> has actual knowledge that the information is related to a <u>veteran's</u> medical debt and the <u>consumer reporting agency</u> is in compliance with its obligation under section 302(c)(5) of the Economic Growth, Regulatory Relief, and Consumer Protection Act.

(b) Exempted cases

The provisions of paragraphs (1) through (5) of subsection (a) are not applicable in the case of any <u>consumer credit</u> report to be used in connection with—

(1) a <u>credit</u> transaction involving, or which may reasonably be expected to involve, a principal amount of $150,000 or more;

(2) the underwriting of life insurance involving, or which may reasonably be expected to involve, a face amount of $150,000 or more; or

(3) the employment of any individual at an annual salary which equals, or which may reasonably be expected to equal $75,000, or more.

(c) Running of reporting period

(1) In general

The 7-year period referred to in paragraphs (4) and (6) of subsection (a) shall begin, with respect to any delinquent <u>account</u> that is placed for collection (internally or by referral to a third party, whichever is earlier), charged to profit and loss, or subjected to any similar action, upon the expiration of the 180-day period beginning on the date of the commencement of the delinquency which immediately preceded the collection activity, charge to profit and loss, or similar action.

(2) EFFECTIVE DATE
Paragraph (1) shall apply only to items of information added to the file of a consumer on or after the date that is 455 days after September 30, 1996.

(d) INFORMATION REQUIRED TO BE DISCLOSED

(1) TITLE 11 INFORMATION
Any consumer reporting agency that furnishes a consumer report that contains information regarding any case involving the consumer that arises under title 11 shall include in the report an identification of the chapter of such title 11 under which such case arises if provided by the source of the information. If any case arising or filed under title 11 is withdrawn by the consumer before a final judgment, the consumer reporting agency shall include in the report that such case or filing was withdrawn upon receipt of documentation certifying such withdrawal.

(2) KEY FACTOR IN CREDIT SCORE INFORMATION
Any consumer reporting agency that furnishes a consumer report that contains any credit score or any other risk score or predictor on any consumer shall include in the report a clear and conspicuous statement that a key factor (as defined in section 1681g(f)(2)(B) of this title) that adversely affected such score or predictor was the number of enquiries, if such a predictor was in fact a key factor that adversely affected such score. This paragraph shall not apply to a check services company, acting as such, which issues authorizations for the purpose of approving or processing negotiable instruments, electronic fund transfers, or similar methods of payments, but only to the extent that such company is engaged in such activities.

(e) INDICATION OF CLOSURE OF ACCOUNT BY CONSUMER
If a consumer reporting agency is notified pursuant to section 1681s–2(a)(4) of this title that a credit account of a consumer was voluntarily closed by the consumer, the agency shall indicate that fact in any consumer report that includes information related to the account.

(f) INDICATION OF DISPUTE BY CONSUMER
If a consumer reporting agency is notified pursuant to section 1681s–2(a)(3) of this title that information regarding a consumer who [1] was furnished to the agency is disputed by the consumer, the agency shall indicate that fact in each consumer report that includes the disputed information.

(g) TRUNCATION OF CREDIT CARD AND DEBIT CARD NUMBERS

(1) IN GENERAL

Except as otherwise provided in this subsection, no person that accepts credit cards or debit cards for the transaction of business shall print more than the last 5 digits of the card number or the expiration date upon any receipt provided to the cardholder at the point of the sale or transaction.

(2) LIMITATION

This subsection shall apply only to receipts that are electronically printed, and shall not apply to transactions in which the sole means of recording a credit card or debit card account number is by handwriting or by an imprint or copy of the card.

(3) EFFECTIVE DATE

This subsection shall become effective—

(A) 3 years after December 4, 2003, with respect to any cash register or other machine or device that electronically prints receipts for credit card or debit card transactions that is in use before January 1, 2005; and

(B) 1 year after December 4, 2003, with respect to any cash register or other machine or device that electronically prints receipts for credit card or debit card transactions that is first put into use on or after January 1, 2005.

(h) NOTICE OF DISCREPANCY IN ADDRESS

(1) IN GENERAL

If a person has requested a consumer report relating to a consumer from a consumer reporting agency described in section 1681a(p) of this title, the request includes an address for the consumer that substantially differs from the addresses in the file of the consumer, and the agency provides a consumer report in response to the request, the consumer reporting agency shall notify the requester of the existence of the discrepancy.

(2) REGULATIONS

(A) Regulations required

The Bureau shall,,[2] in consultation with the Federal banking agencies, the National Credit Union Administration, and the Federal Trade Commission,,[2] prescribe regulations providing guidance regarding reasonable policies and procedures that a user of a consumer report should employ when such user has received a notice of discrepancy under paragraph (1).

(B) Policies and procedures to be included

The regulations prescribed under subparagraph (A) shall describe reasonable policies and procedures for use by a user of a consumer report—

(i) to form a reasonable belief that the user knows the identity of the person to whom the consumer report pertains; and

(ii) if the user establishes a continuing relationship with the consumer, and the user regularly and in the ordinary course of business furnishes information to the consumer reporting agency from which the notice of discrepancy pertaining to the consumer was obtained, to reconcile the address of the consumer with the consumer reporting agency by furnishing such address to such consumer reporting agency as part of information regularly furnished by the user for the period in which the relationship is established.

(Pub. L. 90–321, title VI, § 605, as added Pub. L. 91–508, title VI, § 601, Oct. 26, 1970, 84 Stat. 1129; amended Pub. L. 95–598, title III, § 312(b), Nov. 6, 1978, 92 Stat. 2676; Pub. L. 104–208, div. A, title II, § 2406(a)–(e)(1), Sept. 30, 1996, 110 Stat. 3009–434, 3009–435; Pub. L. 105–347, § 5, Nov. 2, 1998, 112 Stat. 3211; Pub. L. 108–159, title I, § 113, title II, § 212(d), title III, § 315, title IV, § 412(b), (c), title VIII, § 811(c)(1), (2)(A), Dec. 4, 2003, 117 Stat. 1959, 1977, 1996, 2002, 2011; Pub. L. 111–203, title X, § 1088(a)(2)(D), (5), July 21, 2010, 124 Stat. 2087; Pub. L. 115–174, title III, § 302(b)(2), May 24, 2018, 132 Stat. 1333.)

• ABOUT THE AUTHOR

C.A. Knuckles is currently incarcerated in Maryland. He has built Pro Se Prisoner into the go-to financial literacy publishing brand. This new book Pro se Prisoner: Guide to Build Wealth, is the follow-up to his successful Pro se Prisoner: How to Buy Stocks and Bitcoin. Mr. Knuckles goal is to help prisoners build wealth and learn about finances by giving them the knowledge to succeed while sitting in a prison cell. If you have questions or ideas or need advice about business-related matters, including investments, please feel free to contact him through his investment company.

The Attic Group, LLC

1 East Chase Street, Suite #1101

Baltimore, Maryland 21202

Mr. Knuckles would love to get your feedback about the book, make suggestions for the next one, or just let him know you liked it. Write the above address. First, Becoming wealthy requires changing your mindset, obtaining knowledge, and taking action! Thanks for becoming a Pro se Prisoner!

• Other Publications by Author

Pro Se Prisoner Business Planner Forms Included

Pro Se Prisoner How to Build Business Credit Guide

Mindset Poverty vs. Wealthy

Pro Se Prisoner Legally Improve Your Credit

Pro Se Prisoner Business Funding Guide

ORDER BY Phone: 866-582-1982, Online: theatticgroup.org, or Mail SASE (self-addressed stamped envelope) for information and pricing: The Attic Group LLC, 1 East Chase St., Ste. 1101, Baltimore, MD 21202.

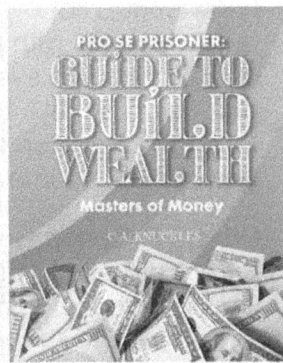

FREEBIRD PUBLISHERS

Thanks for your interest in
Freebird Publishers!

We value our customers and would love to hear from you! Reviews are an important part in bringing you quality publications. We love hearing from our readers-rather it's good or bad (though we strive for the best)!

If you could take the time to review/rate any publication you've purchased with Freebird Publishers we would appreciate it!

If your loved one uses Amazon, have them post your review on the books you've read. This will help us tremendously, in providing future publications that are even more useful to our readers and growing our business.

Amazon works off of a 5 star rating system. When having your loved one rate us be sure to give them your chosen star number as well as a written review. Though written reviews aren't required, we truly appreciate hearing from you.

Sample Review Received on Inmate Shopper

poeticsunshine

⭐⭐⭐⭐⭐ **Truly a guide**

Reviewed in the United States on June 29, 2023

Verified Purchase

This book is a powerhouse of information. My son had to calm/ground himself to prioritize where to start.

CURRENT FULL COLOR CATALOG
92-Pages filled with books, gifts and services for prisoners

We have created four different versions of our new catalog A: Complete B:No Pen Pal Content C:No Sexy Photo Content D:No Pen Pal and Sexy Content. Available in full Color or B&W (please specify) please make sure you order the correct catalog based on your prison mail room regulations. We are not responsible for rejected or lost in the mail catalogs. Send SASE for info on stamp options.

Freebird Publishers Book Selection Includes:

- Ask. Believe. Receive.: Our Power to Create Our Own Destiny
- Celebrity Female Star Power
- Cell Chef 1 & 2
- Cellpreneur: The Millionaire Prisoner's Guidebook
- Chapter 7 Bankruptcy: Seven Steps to Financial Freedom
- Convicted Creations Cookbook
- Cooking With Hot Water
- DIY for Prisoners
- Federal Rules of Criminal Procedures Pocket Guide
- Federal Rules of Evidence Pocket Guide
- Fine Dining Cookbook 1, 2, 3
- Freebird Publisher's Gift Look Book
- Get Money: Self Educate, Get Rich, & Enjoy Life (3 book series)
- Habeas Corpus Manual
- Hobo Pete and the Ghost Train
- Hot Girl Safari: Non-Nude Photo Book
- How to Write a Good Letter From Prison
- Ineffective Assistance of Counsel
- Inmate Shopper
- Inmate Shopper Censored
- Introduction to Financial Success
- Kitty Kat: Adult Entertainment Resource Book

- Life With a Record
- Locked Down Cookin'
- Locked Up Love Letters: Becoming the Perfect Pen Pal
- Parent to Parent: Raising Children from Prison
- Penacon Presents: The Prisoners Guide to Being a Perfect Pen Pal
- Pen Pal Success: The Ultimate Guide to Getting & Keeping Pen Pals
- Pen Pals: A Personal Guide for Prisoners
- Pillow Talk: Adult Non-Nude Photo Book
- Post-Conviction Relief Series (Books 1-7)
- Prison Health Handbook
- Prison Legal Guide
- Prison Picasso
- Prisoner's Communication Guidelines for Navigating in Prison
- Prisonyland Adult Coloring Book
- Pro Se Guide to Legal Research & Writing
- Pro Se Prisoner: How to Buy Stocks and Bitcoin
- Pro Se Section 1983 Manual
- Section 2254 Pro Se Guide to Winning Federal Relief
- Soft Shots: Adult Non-Nude Photo Book
- The Best 500 Non-Profit Organizations for Prisoners & Their Families
- Weight Loss Unlocked
- Write & Get Paid

CATALOG ONLY $5 - SHIPS BY FIRST CLASS MAIL
ADDITIONAL OPTION: add $5 for Shipping and Handling with Tracking

PayPal
MasterCard | VISA | DISCOVER | BANK

NO ORDER FORM NEEDED CLEARLY WRITE ON PAPER & SEND PAYMENT TO:
FREEBIRD PUBLISHERS 221 Pearl St., Ste. 541, North Dighton, MA 02764
www.FreebirdPublishers.com Diane@FreebirdPublishers.com Text/Phone: 774-406-8682
We accept all forms of payment. Plus Venmo & CashApp! Venmo: @FreebirdPublishers CashApp: $FreebirdPublishers

www.ingramcontent.com/pod-product-compliance
Lightning Source LLC
Chambersburg PA
CBHW071958220326
41599CB00032BA/6548